EPISTLES TO THE APOSTLE

Tarsus–Please Forward

Colin Morris

ABINGDON
PRESS
Nashville
New York

EPISTLES TO THE APOSTLE

Copyright © 1974 by Colin Morris.
First printed in Great Britain by Hodder and Stoughton,
Limited, 1974.

ISBN 0-687-11989-8

MANUFACTURED BY THE PARTHENON PRESS AT
NASHVILLE, TENNESSEE, UNITED STATES OF AMERICA

Contents

Introduction

It is probably an appalling confession for a Christian minister to make, but until comparatively recently, Paul had for me a lack of fascination all his own. The seemingly endless passages of closely reasoned argument concerned with issues such as circumcision which are without relevance to our time; the apparent egotism; the censoriousness, relieved only by odd prose poems of great lyrical beauty sparkling like diamonds in a mountain of sludge— Paul's Epistles just weren't for me. Though I must confess that when I needed an ingenious text to nail to the masthead of a sermonic theme, Paul had his uses.

I was a Jesus-man, straight down the line. And I possibly bore a subconscious grudge against Paul who seemed to have been the Galilean carpenter's fanatical stage manager—transforming a way of life so unfettered as a soaring bird into an ordered, organized, and juiceless religion. I wonder if the old Jewish tentmaker will ever forgive me?

My conversion came about when I made a simple realization—the second third of the New Testament for which I held Paul responsible was neither a theological treatise nor the rule-book of the early church. It consisted of letters written by a man! Such a discovery hardly qualifies one for the Nobel Prize. Any Sunday school child could have whispered the fact in my ear. But I was making encouraging progress. For correspondence is rarely one-sided. Since Paul wrote letters, he must also have received and answered letters in return.

The problem is obvious. We have at least some of Paul's letters to early churches; nowhere is there any record of the replies he received, though there are passages in some Epistles which appear to have been inspired by queries addressed to him or charges made against him. But they have vanished without trace. Paul, unlike the modern church bureaucrat, did not leave behind him a legacy of endless filing cabinets.

So I invented some letters to Paul—a confession which embarrasses me somewhat; Heaven knows why! It would have been insufferable arrogance to fabricate letters purporting to come *from* Paul, whereas any half-wit could have written *to* him, and some probably did.

So far so good. But any first-year theological student is aware that the Pauline corpus (as they say) is a veritable minefield of scholastic pitfalls—dating, destination, even authorship. In the end I decided to settle for an enlightened fundamentalism—avoid Hebrews like the plague, and assume that the rest of the letters, including Ephesians and the Pastorals, were written by Paul or someone else of the same name. After all, New Testiment scholars are, like most intellectuals, cannibals. They'll eat alive one of their own tribe who steps out of line, but would hardly deign to sharpen their teeth on a run-of-the-mill parson who can honorably plead guilty but insane to charges of Pauline mutilation. Anyway, New Testament scholars are unlikely to read this book; firstly, because it isn't written in German; secondly, because it isn't a Ph.D. dissertation; and thirdly, because it is essentially a *jeu d'esprit*—and we all know how serious serious scholars are!

A more formidable difficulty was that the most apposite answer Paul might have given to a conjectural letter could be made up of bits of a number of different epistles. Here, I felt on safer ground. I might not be a Pauline scholar; but then, neither was Paul. Like me he was a missionary and preacher. And which preacher, good, bad, or indifferent, having polished a sermon until it shone like a little light in a naughty world, has not used it again and again? And why not? If the grandeur delusion may be forgiven, the preacher is in the same case as a Beethoven or a Bach, who surely did not compose their music to be played *once*. By the same token Paul's hymn to love in Corinthians and his affirmation of the cosmic lordship of Christ in Philippians, to mention but two examples among many, are so superb that he must have used them whenever the occasion was appropriate, possibly as circular letters to a number of churches and individuals.

So then, using that license permitted to the Christian publicist but denied to the scholar, who dare not mention the day of the week in one of his writings without a footnote justifying it, I have hacked Paul's letters about while trying honestly to avoid major historical errors. I doubt that I have succeeded, but I would beg the indulgence of Paulinists who might agree that it is more important for Paul to come alive in a generation which finds him forbiddingly remote than to achieve a scholastic exactitude which is beyond me. After all, it is the contents of the letters, not the critical problems associated with them, which have converting power.

The purist is sure to come across the odd term or expression which is strictly anachronistic. I took the risk of including such words knowingly, in the belief that it was more important to anchor Paul and his correspondents firmly in our time than to use terminology which had no point of reference in the mind of the twentieth-century reader. The translators of the New English Bible must also have thought the same. They occasionally include expressions and terms which are modern equivalents of those to be found in the original language. And what was good enough for the late, great, and revered C. H. Dodd and his colleagues is good enough for me.

Though I claim the right to exercise sanctified imagination, I must acknowledge my indebtedness to New Testament scholars whose commentaries have shed light on issues and controversies very much to the fore in Paul's time but now lost in the mists of antiquity. Two works in particular were immensely valuable. Dr. Sydney Cave's *The Gospel of Paul* (Hodder), though it was published in 1928, I selected from other similar works because it puts the teaching of Paul in a missionary context—which is just where I needed it to be. Equally important was the first volume of Hans Lietzmann's monumental study of Christian origins, *The Beginnings of the Christian Church.* It is reassuring in a time of ecclesiastical confusion and uncertainty to learn that the early Church was also in a state of holy chaos for long periods—and survived!

So much for the letters to Paul. Those from Paul are taken from Scripture. One is not permitted to play fast and loose with that book. But there is a wide choice of translations and paraphrases. I have almost entirely used J. B. Phillips's *Letters to Young Churches* in the 1957 Macmillan edition. To Dr. Phillips I owe an unrepayable debt for clothing Paul in flesh and blood and making me appreciate that he was not only a giant in the church's history but also a great human being. I must make it plain however that the passages from Paul which appear in this book are often compilations of my own choosing from different sections of Dr. Phillips's translation, and obviously he bears no responsibility for my vagaries. I hope he will not feel that I have treated his work in a cavalier manner. If he should, quite legitimately, take such a view then I can only ask his forgiveness on the grounds that though my scholarship has been defective my motives were honorable.

I cannot reiterate too strongly that I have sometimes used sentences and phrases taken from a number of different parts of Dr. Phillips's translation to make up a single Pauline reply to one of my invented letters. I hope therefore that in fairness to Dr. Phillips any reader wishing to quote from his translation will do so from his own published version and not from my cannibalized variant of it.

I first worked out the idea of a two-way correspondence with Paul for a series of BBC *Thoughts for the Day,* and I am grateful to Peter de Rosa, who was at that time my producer, for suggestions and criticisms which I have carried over into the printed version. My thanks are due to Pauline Webb who cast a critical eye over the text and suggested rearrangements of the material and the occasional omission. I hope to be given the privilege of doing a similar hatchet job on one of her books some day! I am also indebted to Jean Palk for typing the manuscript as well as coping with a dozen other jobs at the same time.

Colin M. Morris

1

In the Beginning Was the End

Well, what would *you* do if you had it on the highest
authority that the world was about to come to an end at
any moment? The earliest Christian communities must
have been in a fair state of chaos. What ought they to do
about their property and possessions? Paul must have been
deluged with anxious inquiries. For instance:

A Thessalonian Businessman to Paul

My dear Paul,

The followers of Jesus in this city are in receipt of
your letter which was read out in church a month ago
and which appears to confirm a widely held view here
that our Lord will be returning in glory at any moment
to take believers such as my humble self back with him
to heaven. Being a hard-headed businessman I took your
words with the utmost seriousness. To prepare myself

and my family for the Day of the Lord, I sold my business at a knock-down price and gave the proceeds to the poor—and that, let me add, was a tidy sum, but I assume we won't need cash in heaven!

So here I am with my bags packed, my property disposed of, and myself, my wife, and my children taking it in shifts to scan the skies for something unusual to appear. In fact, every time I hear a trumpet, I nearly jump out of my skin! And what has happened? Nothing.

I can't help feeling that I've been made to look an utter fool in the eyes of my friends and business acquaintances. They all think I've gone stark, raving mad. Meanwhile, the man who bought my business, far from suffering the catastrophe reserved for the wicked, is making a handsome profit and living in my house, which is one of the finest in the city. He is allowing us to camp at the bottom of my, or rather his, garden, with passersby leaning over the fence gaping at us and making the most offensive remarks. Not a pleasant predicament for a former mayor to be in. Not that earthly honors matter, of course. But one has one's legitimate pride.

Would you kindly tell me what I do next? The tax people are pestering me for last year's assessment, and I haven't a lead shekel to pay them with. Being a man of God you are probably unaware that disposing of one's assets in the interests of a religion which is not recognized by the state does not qualify one for retrospective tax exemption. So I'm in a pretty pickle, let me tell you!

I feel most strongly that the financial implications of the Second Coming should have been given more serious consideration by the apostles—though I suppose tentmakers like yourself and former fishermen and so on could hardly be expected to appreciate the ramifications of big business. Indeed, I doubt that your incomes are substantial enough to attract any tax at all. How fortunate you are!

I am in a most embarrassing situation, what with a nagging wife and three children who have gotten completely out of hand because they prefer earthly pranks to what they imagine will be heavenly boredom. You don't need me to tell you that we Christians in Thessalonica have suffered much persecution. But it is one thing to suffer for the faith; quite another to be made to look ridiculous.

However, I do not intend to move from this spot until Jesus comes to collect me. Meanwhile it would be quite dishonest of me not to express grave concern at the most unbusinesslike way in which this whole matter is being dealt with.

I await an early reply, otherwise I shall be forced to turn the whole matter over to my lawyers.

Paphlos
formerly Managing Director
Paphlos Importers Limited

Beware of Pre-Parousia Paralysis!

We do implore you, by the very certainty of Christ's coming and of our meeting him together, to keep your heads and not be thrown off your balance by any prediction or message or letter purporting to come from us, and saying that the day of Christ is almost here. That day will not come before there arises a definite rejection of God and the appearance of the Lawless Man. We gave you this principle to work on: "If a man will not work, he shall not eat." Now we hear that you have some among you living quite undisciplined lives, never doing a stroke of work. Our order to such men, indeed our appeal by the Lord Jesus Christ, is to settle down to work and eat the food they have earned themselves. Don't get tired of honest work! The Lord is utterly to be trusted by all who have faith in him.

Paphlos was not appeased by Paul's reply. Jesus did not make a special journey to collect him, so the worthy gentleman huffed and puffed his way down to his lawyers, from whom Paul received the following letter:

Flaccus and Florus, Attorneys at Law, to Paul

Dear Sir,

Our client, Mr. T. E. Paphlos, former Managing Director of Paphlos Importers Ltd., has referred to us the matter of the disposal of his considerable assets on the strength of your personal assurance that he would shortly be taken up into a state referred to, we understand, as "Heaven," in which we further understand money and other valuables are unnecessary. It is not our purpose to engage in theological controversy with you about the existence of any such place or the conditions of life pertaining thereto. We are, however, instructed that our client, who is a gentleman of considerable standing in the community, having been exposed to ridicule, wrote to you and received by way of reply a general circular advising all in his situation to work for a living.

In our view Mr. Paphlos has been the victim of a fraudulent deception, and we are instructed by him to require you to make good your promise regarding this "Heaven" within thirty days, or we shall be forced to take further action to obtain compensation for our client in order that he may resume the style of life to which he has accustomed before he fell under your influence.

Yours, etc.
Flaccus & Florus

Mr. Paphlos and his lawyers, no doubt to their chagrin, got only the dubious satisfaction of becoming sermon illustrations. As Paul was at pains to point out again and again, no human financial sacrifice could possibly compare to the unimaginable change of status willingly accepted by Jesus for our sakes.

Some Investment Advice

Do you remember the generosity of Jesus Christ, the Lord of us all? He was rich beyond our telling, yet he became poor for your sakes so that his poverty might make you rich. The important thing is to be willing to give as much as we can—that is what God accepts. It is a matter of share and share alike.

Tell those who are rich in this present world not to be contemptuous of others, and not to rest the weight of their confidence on the transitory power of wealth but on the living God, who generously gives us everything for our enjoyment. Their security should be invested in the life to come, so that they may be sure of holding a share in the life which is permanent.

Paul was not an easy man to browbeat, so Paphlos' fate would finally be decided, not in the law courts, but upon his grasp of a simple truth that is at the heart of the gospel. Having rid himself of his earthly wealth in expectation of heavenly glory, would he have the humility to receive from others; to accept what he had been accustomed to giving; to become dependent upon his fellow Christians at the expense of his pride? It wouldn't be easy for the ex-mayor of Thessalonica to place himself at the mercy of people he had probably thought of as socially inferior. But what excellent practice it would be for developing the grace to accept God's grace!

Other anxious inquiries came from those who wanted to know what would be the fate of their non-Christian friends, or even that of their fellow Christians, who had died before Christ appeared. For instance:

Crestus to Paul

Greetings from a humble workman! Something is worrying me a lot. My wife and I were eagerly waiting for our Lord's return in glory. I was ready to down tools at a moment's notice, and I still am. But something terrible has happened. My wife died last week. She was a good Christian woman and put up cheerfully with hardship and persecution for Jesus' sake.

My question is this: Must I leave her in the ground when I am taken bodily up into heaven, if I am thought worthy of that honor? It would break my heart. And I am not alone in my pain. There are many Christians here whose loved ones will not have lived to see the dawning of the Day of the Lord.

May I respectfully ask you to deal with this matter when you write again to us in Thessalonica? You will earn the eternal gratitude of

Crestus, the Ironsmith

Die in Christ and You Are Safe!

We don't want you, my brothers, to be in any doubt about those who "fall asleep" in death, or to grieve over them like men who have no hope. After all, if we believe that Jesus died and rose again from death, then we can believe that God will just as surely bring with Jesus all who are "asleep" in him. Those who are still living when he comes will not in any way precede those who have previously fallen asleep. Those who have died in Christ will be the first to rise, and then we who are still living on the earth will be swept up with them into the clouds to meet the Lord in the air. The trumpet will sound, and the dead shall be raised beyond the reach of corruption, and we who are still alive shall suddenly be utterly changed.

Meanwhile, Paul's in-tray was filling up with letters, some of which were cranky or raised trivial issues he hadn't time or inclination to answer. For example:

Pontus to Paul

I wonder if you could clear up one point for me relating to our Lord's return and our journey with him to heaven? My mother-in-law lives with us and, frankly, makes my life a living hell. Jesus himself said that there are many mansions in heaven. Can I be assured that she will have separate accommodation, preferably in an entirely different wing? Otherwise, I'm just not going. Much as I believe the gospel, I would infinitely prefer the oblivion of the Jewish Sheol to the eternal yakking of her voice!

Or this:

Simpius to Paul

In a recent sermon you gave to the Christians at Thessalonica, you referred to our "meeting the Lord in the air." It almost made my stomach turn over! You see I've no head for heights. I don't suppose you could use your influence with Above (ugh! the very word makes me giddy!) to arrange some other method of getting into heaven? If not, I'll just have to get the pharmacist to fix me up (there's that awful word again!) some elixir. But I can't spend from now till then doped to the eyebrows on the off-chance, can I?

To prove I'm not being frivolous, let me tell you that

19

every time we hear in church that story of our Lord being taken by the devil to the pinnacle of the Temple, I faint dead away!

Then there is this intriguing letter:

Paul from Johannes Robinsonensis

I suspect that like everyone else around here, you'll think I'm balmy, but I am working on a theory that the earth is *round*. Now, go on and laugh! You may say, Everyone knows it's flat, but I reply, Where's your evidence? Have you ever heard of anyone falling over the edge of it? You have traveled by sea more than most people, and I firmly believe that if you sailed on and on you would eventually arrive at the port from which you first set out.

You may wonder what all this has to do with religion rather than science, but I have a feeling that you will get my point, which is that I reject utterly the three-decker cosmology—heaven above, earth in the middle, and hell below. If I am right, then it makes nonsense to talk about a God "up there" or "meeting the Lord in the air." Indeed, my instinct tells me that you yourself were being poetic rather than literal when you wrote of being "caught up in the third heaven."

I am busy working on an entirely new approach to theology. Honest to God, as soon as I get out of this asylum, I intend to write a book that will shake the whole Christian world.

> Respectfully,
> † Johannes Robinsonensis

P.S. Any chance of your writing a preface to my book?

There is no record of Paul making any comment on the good Johannes' startling theory that the earth was round

—so startling an idea that he was confined to a mental institution for the mortal offense of being too far ahead of his time. But Paul did send the bishop copies of extracts from his letters to various churches which showed that he did not believe in a God to be found solely in one dimension—upwards—but at work everywhere in the world. He even advanced an idea so revolutionary that it would have qualified him for the padded cell next to Johannes Robinsonensis—that Christ was God's agent in creation and held the universe together by his power:

The Glory of the Cosmic Christ

There is one Lord, one faith, one baptism, one God, one Father of us all, who is the one over all, the one working through all and the one living in all.

And I pray that you, firmly fixed in love yourselves, may be able to grasp (with all Christians) how wide and deep and long and high is the love of Christ. Now Christ is the visible expression of the invisible God. He existed before creation began, for it was through him that everything was made, whether spiritual or material, seen or unseen. Through him, and for him, also, were created power and dominion, ownership and authority. In fact, every single thing was created through, and for, him. He is both the first principle and the upholding principle of the whole scheme of creation.

cc. Johannes Robinsonensis

It must be admitted that Paul was not entirely consistent on this question of the exact timing of the expected Day of the Lord. He was, after all, a missionary and not a theologian. He lived by revelation rather than systematic study in some university library. God was always surprising him, not by planting profound ideas in his head, but by subjecting him to a bewildering range of experiences. So his predictions about the dating of the Second Advent oscillated wildly between "soon" and "not yet." Depending possibly on the degree of danger he was facing, he was never quite sure whether he would be alive or dead when the Lord returned in glory. Hence, assorted snippets which seem somewhat contradictory:

I May Be Dead or Alive When Jesus Returns—It Does Not Matter

Listen, and I will tell you a secret. We shall not all die, but suddenly, in the twinkling of an eye, everyone of us will be changed as the trumpet sounds! The trumpet will sound, and the dead shall be raised beyond the reach of corruption, and we who are still alive shall suddenly be utterly changed.

But:

We should like you, our brothers, to know something of what we went through in Asia. At that time we were completely overwhelmed, the burden was more than we could bear, in fact we told ourselves that this was the end. Yet we believe now that we had this experience of coming to the end of our tether that we might learn to trust, not in ourselves, but in God who can raise the dead.

It's nice to know that Paul was not infallible and that his faith did not lack the tinge of doubt which makes it an adventure to believe. The question about whether he would be alive or dead when the Day of the Lord dawned —that tension between "soon" and "not yet"—resolved itself when he realized that, as he wrote to the church in Rome:

22

The truth is that we neither live nor die as self-contained units. At every turn life links us to God, and when we die we come face to face with him. In life or death we are in the hands of God.

One man, however, was alarmed by Paul's joyous sense of abandon, the loss of his needless fretting as to whether he would be alive to greet the Lord on his glorious return. Not being a theologian, this simple man did not see in Paul's changed attitude to the Day of the Lord the final rooting out of Jewish apocalyptic notions by mature Christian hope. This man was the prison officer of Philippi who was converted by Paul and Silas while they were in his charge. He feared that Paul, once more in jail in Rome, was becoming "prison-happy"—a condition about which he knew much. So he felt constrained to send Paul a note of warning:

Prison Officer Stachys to Paul

My dear Paul,

I'm smuggling this note in to you through one of my pals who works in the prison at Rome. I am worried by some of the things you have been writing recently. As you know, I have great experience of prisoners, and after a long time in a cell they start to go mad. At first they are depressed and prowl around like caged animals. Then slowly they seem to stop being part of the real world. They become what we call "prison-happy" and lose all interest in everything except their food ration. Sometimes they mumble to themselves, talking utter nonsense. Others stare at the walls for hours on end. You mean so much to all of us who are your spiritual children. I pray constantly for your release. I know that God works in miraculous ways, and it may be that another earthquake like the one that frightened me to death at Philippi will smash down the walls of your cell. But tradition has it that a learned rabbi claimed that God never does the same thing twice, and I fear this may be so in your case. Of course we know that when Jesus returns you will have the freedom of the City of Heaven. But when will that be? Your happiness seems, well, unnatural. How can anyone be happy in a stinking, damp, dark jail cell? Do please keep a grip on yourself for all our sakes. I enclose some writing materials in the hope you might occupy your time in setting down your experiences.

Forgive my presumption in writing to you. Compared to you I am an infant in the faith, but I do know a lot about prisons! Lydia asks me to send you her love.

Stachys

Joy in Jail!

Christ is being preached . . . and that fact makes me very happy. Yes, and I shall go on being very happy, for I know that what is happening will be for the good of my own soul, thanks to your prayers and the resources of the Spirit of Jesus Christ. It all accords with my own earnest wishes and hopes, which are that I should never be in any way ashamed, but that now, as always, I should honor Christ with the utmost boldness by the way I live, whether that means I am to face death or to go on living. For living to me means simply "Christ," and if I die I should merely gain more of him. I have everything I want—in fact I am rich. Yes, I am quite content.

Paul had other serious problems to deal with. There was, for example, the question of marriage. It is difficult to sustain the case that he was a woman-hater. Many of his friends were women, and in his letters he sends greetings

to them—Lydia, Phoebe, Prisca, Tryphaena and Try-
phosa, Persis, Julia, and the sister of Nereus, Mary, who
was a tower of strength in Rome. A more likely explanation is that Paul believed his generation or the one after
it was likely to be the last on earth, in which case why
alter the *status quo* and add the complication of children
whose existence would be an added source of anxiety
during the terrible world catastrophe that he thought
would precede the end?

You Could Do Worse Than Marry

*My opinion is this, that amid the difficulties of the
present time you would do best to remain just as you
are. Are you married? Well, don't try to be separated.
Are you unattached? Then don't try to get married. But
if you, a man, should marry, don't think that you have
done anything sinful. And the same applies to a young
woman. Yet I do believe that those who take this step
are bound to find the married state an extra burden in
these critical days, and I should like you to be as unen-
cumbered as possible. There is no time to indulge in
sorrow, no time for enjoying our joys; those who buy
have no time to enjoy their possessions, and indeed their
every contact with the world must be as light as possible,
for the present scheme of things is rapidly passing away.
That is why I should like you to be as free from worldly
entanglements as possible.*

Thaddeus' Son to Paul

I love a girl whose father is an elder of the church
here and absolutely forbids us to marry because you
have ruled against it—something to do with the end of
the world approaching, so he tells me. Well, I am not
a Christian. I do not believe the end of the world *is*

approaching. I am a student of philosophy, and frankly I find the antics of the Christian community here utterly ridiculous. Well, that's their affair, but when it affects my own life and causes bitter unhappiness to my girl, then it seems to me it is time you thought this question of marriage through more deeply. I find your writings on this subject sometimes obscure; at other times completely contradictory. I am a disciple of Seneca, the great Stoic, so you will appreciate where I stand on this matter. While condemning adultery as a form of theft, he finds nothing immoral in an unmarried couple sleeping together. No doubt you are familiar with his *Controv. II,* where he defends a young man accused of immorality and writes: "He has not sinned; he loves a prostitute; that is usual; he is young, he will amend his faults and marry a wife." My girl is not a prostitute. We are both young, healthy, and passionate, and I think it intolerable that we should be forced to conform to your cranky ideas on social ethics, based as they are on a mish-mash of Jewish apocalyptic concepts combined with the dubious teachings of the Nazarene. You are not even consistent about this so-called Day of the Lord —a theory which no reputable scholar to my knowledge takes seriously. One moment you say "it's at hand," the next that it will not occur until all the Jews have been saved. Some hope of that!

Hadn't you better give some clear guidance to your followers at Corinth? To put it mildly, their personal relationships are a shambles. Meanwhile, though according to my personal beliefs I should be doing nothing wrong in sleeping with my girl whatever her father says, I have no desire to grieve him, so I'm prepared to wait and see if any guidance that an intelligent man as opposed to a drunken Corinthian sailor can take seriously is forthcoming from you.

Thaddeus II

More About Marriage . . .

Now let me deal with the questions raised in your letter. It is a good principle for a man to have no physical contact with women. Nevertheless, because casual liaisons are so prevalent, let every man have his own wife and every woman her own husband. I think it is far better for them to be married than to be tortured by unsatisfied desire. For a brother who has a non-Christian wife who is willing to live with him he should not divorce her. For the unbelieving husband is, in a sense, consecrated by being joined to the person of his wife; the unbelieving wife is similarly "consecrated" by the Christian brother she has married. If this were not so then your children would bear the stains of paganism, whereas they are actually consecrated to God. This is my advice, though it is not a divine command.

There was, however, another complication with which Paul had to deal. This was the custom for a Christian man to live with a virgin in a relationship like that of brother and sister—"spiritual marriage," in fact. Human nature being what it is, sexual drives were putting such liaisons under great strain, so Paul felt it right to deal with this matter also in the same letter:

. . . But I Think Christian Friendship Is Better

If any man feels he is not behaving honorably towards the woman he loves, especially as she is beginning to lose her first youth and the emotional strain is considerable, let him do what his heart tells him to do—let them be married, there is no sin in that. Yet for the man of steadfast purpose who is able to bear the strain and has his own desires well under control; if he decides not to marry the young woman, he too will be doing the right thing. Both of them are right, one in

*marrying and the other in refraining from marriage, but
the latter has chosen the better of two right courses.*

Closely related to the question of the end of the world
was that great mystery which has baffled men from the
beginning of time—what is their fate after death? In
Thessalonica where Christians waited with bated breath
for the glorious return of Jesus, their main worry as we
have seen was not so much with their own fate—they expected to be taken up into heaven while still alive—but
with the destiny of loved ones who had died during the
time of waiting. In Corinth Paul found himself in a more
complicated wrangle. All kinds of ideas were flying around.
The Epicureans denied the immortality of the soul. The
Stoics weren't sure. The Platonists had no doubt about
the immortality of the soul. The great Seneca referred to
any form of survival beyond death as a "lovely dream."
The traditional Jewish concept that the bodies of the dead
would be raised from the grave at the resurrection had
become confused with Paul's own teaching that the resurrection of Jesus was a guarantee of the resurrection of
individual believers. So the letters must have poured in on
Paul thick and fast:

Paul, from a Very Sick Man

Dear Paul,
    I haven't the strength to write you a long letter.
Anyway, my question is straightforward. My doctor has
told me that I have only a few weeks to live. I am a
recent convert to the faith, and the church elders who
have been most kind in visiting and praying with me
just don't seem able to agree about the matter which
naturally occupies my mind most of all now—death
and after. They either evade my questions or give me

conflicting answers. So I ask you. What will happen to me when I die? I am afraid.

Justus

Alive or Dead—We Are in Christ

Can anything separate us from the love of Christ? Can trouble, pain, or persecution? Can lack of clothes and food, danger to life and limb, the threat of force of arms? No, in all these things we win an overwhelming victory through him who has proved his love for us. I have become absolutely convinced that neither death nor life, neither messenger of heaven nor monarch of earth, neither what happens today nor what may happen tomorrow, neither a power from on high nor a power from below, nor anything else in God's whole world has any power to separate us from the love of God in Jesus Christ our Lord!

Crispus to Paul

My dear Paul,

Possibly because I was the Chief Official of the Synagogue before I was converted by your preaching, the Jewish Christians here have asked me to write to you on this question of the resurrection of the body. Our Greek opponents find the whole idea crude and materialistic. They claim that it brings the soul back into bondage to the body. On the other hand, there is a powerful faction among our members who seem to me to have reverted to Judaism. This very Lord's Day, the preacher took his text from Daniel 12:2—you remember: "Many of those who sleep in the dust of the earth will awake, some to everlasting life, and some to the reproach of eternal abhorrence." We must have this matter cleared up. It is dividing our community and making us laughingstocks to the Greeks and others who scoff that we don't know *what* we believe about immortality. What we need is an authoritative statement from you which will answer both those who deny the resurrection of the body and those who still cling to crude Jewish notions about it.

Justus died last week, at peace and trusting in the Lord Jesus. I'm sure your letter helped him greatly. Now please help us!

Crispus

This Is What Resurrection Means

I passed on to you Corinthians first of all the message I had myself received—that Christ died for our sins, as the Scriptures said he would; that he was buried and rose again on the third day, again as the Scriptures foretold. Now if the rising of Christ from the dead is the very heart of our message, how can some of you deny that there is any resurrection? If Christ is not risen then neither our preaching nor your faith has any meaning at all. For if the dead do not rise neither did Christ rise, and if Christ did not rise your faith is futile and your sins have never been forgiven. Moreover those who have died believing in Christ are utterly dead and gone.

But the glorious fact is that Christ did rise from the dead: he has become the very first to rise of all who sleep the sleep of death. As death entered the world through a man, so has rising from the dead come to us through a man! As members of a sinful race all men die: as members of the Christ of God shall all men be raised to life, each in his proper order. But perhaps someone will ask, "How is the resurrection achieved? With what sort of body do the dead arrive?" Now that is talking without using your minds! In your own ex-

*perience you know that a seed does not germinate with-
out "dying" itself. When you sow a seed you do not sow
the "body" that will eventually be produced. God gives
the seed a "body" according to his laws—a different
"body" to each kind of seed. The body is "sown" in dis-
honor; it is raised in splendor. It is sown in weakness;
it is raised in power. It is sown a natural body; it is
raised a spiritual body. I assure you, my brothers, it is
utterly impossible for flesh and blood to possess the
Kingdom of God. The transitory could never possess
the everlasting. These bodies which are mortal must
be wrapped in immortality. So when the perishable is
lost in the imperishable, the mortal lost in the immor-
tal, this saying will come true: Death is swallowed up
in victory. And so, brothers of mine, stand firm! Let
nothing move you as you busy yourselves in the Lord's
work.*

But Paul, the working missionary, driven by a sense of
mission that amounted to an obsession to introduce men
to the living Christ, had neither time nor inclination to
indulge in mystical speculation about the Beyond. For him,
the context of "death" and "life" was not confined to the
grave but to the spiritual condition of believers and unbelievers in the ongoing activity of the world:

Wake Up—and Live!

*To you, who were spiritually dead all the time that
you drifted along on the stream of this world's ideas
of living, and obeyed its unseen ruler (who is still operating in those who do not respond to the truth of God),
to you Christ has given life! We all lived like that in
the past, and followed the impulses and imaginations
of our evil nature, being in fact under the wrath of*

*God by nature, like everyone else. But even though we
were dead in our sins God was so rich in mercy that
he gave us the very life of Christ (for it is, remember,
by grace and not by achievement that you are saved),
and has lifted us right out of the old life to take our
place with him in Christ in the heavens.*

Paul's conviction that the Day of the Lord was imminent led some young radicals to assume that he was a
supporter of the secular *status quo* when in fact many of
the structures of society were a matter of supreme indifference to him since he believed they would shortly be
transcended. As time wore on and the old persisted,
he was forced to come to terms with some of these issues,
but in the early years of the existence of the Christian
communities, he felt they should order their corporate
lives to prepare for God's new order, compared to which
the ethics of secular society were irrelevant:

Stay Put and Be Content

*The great thing is to obey the orders of Almighty
God. Everyone should stick to the calling in which he
heard the call of God. Were you a slave when you heard
the call? Don't let that worry you, though if you find
the opportunity to become free you had better take it.
But a slave who is called to life in Christ is set free in
the eyes of God. And a man who is free when God calls
him becomes a slave—to Christ himself! My brothers,
let every one of us continue to live his life with God in
the state in which he was when he was called.*

Paul's belief that distinctions between masters and
slaves were of no significance if both were Christ's "free-

men" must, in fairness, be seen as a counsel of perfection which was likely to be less of a burden on masters than on their slaves, as Timon pointed out:

Timon, a Slave, to Paul

My Master,

There is much talk of revolt in this city among slaves, and some among our number have laid plans which have not yet come to anything because of constant quarreling about who should lead the revolt and whether we should escape by sea or land and where we should go to. I myself am not low-born. I became a slave when I was unable to pay a debt, and I work for a master who recognizes my original status and who, though not a Christian, treats me well. It is widely spoken of by hotheads that the religion of Jesus has little concern for freedom and justice and that you, as a Roman citizen, have no desire to overturn the social order. I know this is not so, but I despair of convincing my brothers in bondage. It is not easy to assure a man whose back has been torn to ribbons with the lash that he is a "freeman in Christ"; and what of old men put to death because they are too weak to work? This is a common practice on the great landed estates in the country. Everything I have read of your letters persuades me that you would never encourage Christians to take up arms in the struggle against slavery. But could you not at least use your influence to get Christian slaveowners, some of whom are stern to the point of cruelty with their slaves, to treat them better? Or could you not ask Christians of power and influence in the community to petition the authorities to draw up a Slaves' Charter, ordering all slaveowners to treat their slaves more kindly? I hope to receive manumission shortly, but I have concern for those who must remain in chains for the rest of their lives.

Timon

Paul was unrelenting for two reasons. Firstly, his conviction was that the end of the age was so near that class and caste distinctions were irrelevant—certainly not worth distracting Christians from their spiritual concerns by turning them into reformist pressure groups. Paul was certainly not unfeeling about the suffering of slaves and the like; after all, he had gone the whole gamut of human tribulation from imprisonment, beating, and the nerve-racking experience of being under sentence of death to shipwreck and hunger. There was nothing short of death a slave could suffer he had not shared. And in the end he also paid the ultimate penalty for his faith. The second reason was that he took with the utmost seriousness Jesus' command that "whoever would be first, must become a slave": hence, slavery was a badge of honor rather than a symbol of degradation. For him, there was no essential distinction between a freeman and a slave. A freeman was "the slave of Christ," a Christian slave was a "freeman of the Lord." He stated his position clearly in a number of aphorisms contained in various letters:

All for One, and One for All

We look at it like this: if one died for all men then, in a sense, they all died, and his purpose in dying for them is that their lives now should be no longer lived for themselves but for him who died and rose again for them. This means that our knowledge of men can no longer be based on their outward lives.

The Scripture says: "Whosoever believes in him shall not be disappointed." And that "whosoever" means

anyone, *without distinction. For all have the same Lord,*
whose boundless resources are available to all who turn
to him in faith. For: Whosoever shall call on the name
of the Lord shall be saved.

All of you who were baptized "into" Christ have put
on the family likeness of Christ. Gone is the distinction
between Jew and Greek, slave and free man, male and
female—you are all one in Christ Jesus!

Let Christ himself be your example as to what your
attitude should be. For he, who had always been God
by nature, did not cling to his prerogatives as God's
equal, but stripped himself of all privilege by consenting
to be a slave by nature and being born as mortal man.
And, having become man, he humbled himself by living
a life of utter obedience, even to the extent of dying,
and the death he died was the death of a common
criminal.

And he added this advice to slaves as part of a general
description of the discipline of the new life in Christ:

A Word to Slaves—and a Warning to Their Masters

Slaves, your job is to obey your masters, not with the
idea of currying favor, but as a sincere expression of
your devotion to God. Whatever you do, put your whole
heart and soul into it, as into work done for God, and
not merely for men—knowing that your real reward, a
heavenly one, will come from God, since you are actu-
ally employed by Christ, and not just your earthly
master.

But the slacker and the thief will be judged by God
himself, who naturally has no distinction to make
between master and man. Remember, then, you em-
ployers, that your responsibility is to be fair and just

towards those whom you employ, never forgetting that you yourselves have a Heavenly Employer.

So though Paul was no first-century human rights crusader, in effect he undercut slavery by giving dignity to work, no matter how menial it might appear to men. He invested earthly labor with heavenly status. And he practiced what he preached by befriending the runaway slave, Onesimus, who had robbed his rich master, Philemon, and fled to Rome where he met Paul and was converted. Paul, in prison, would have gladly kept Onesimus by his side as a friend, but he sent him back with a covering letter which reveals Paul's total lack of any sense of social superiority towards slaves:

An Appeal to an Old Friend

This is a simple personal appeal from Paul the old man, in prison for Jesus Christ's sake. I am appealing for my child. Yes I have become a father though I have been under lock and key, and the child's name is— Onesimus! Oh, I know you have found him pretty useless in the past but he is going to be useful now, to both of us. I am sending him back to you: will you receive him as my son, part of me? *I should have dearly loved to have kept him with me.*

It occurs to me that there has been a purpose in your losing him. You lost him, a slave, for a time; now you are having him back for good, not merely a slave, but as a brother Christian. He is already especially loved by me—how much more will you be able to love him, both as a man and as a fellow Christian! You and I have so much in common, haven't we? Then do welcome him as you would welcome me. If you feel he has wronged or cheated you put it down to my account. I, Paul, hereby promise to repay you.

Philemon to Paul

Dearest Paul,

I got your letter safely, together with the useful one
—Onesimus—who brought it. I cannot believe the
change that has come over him! Nor can any other
members of the church here at Colossae. He is living
proof of your claim that any man in Christ is truly a
new man. He has become a tireless Christian evangelist,
and I am honored to treat him not as a slave but as
a friend because he is your friend. Though as far as I
am concerned he can go free, he insists on serving me
with diligence and loyalty. It's almost embarrassing!
He is rapidly becoming a leader in the church here, and
I have no doubt that, taking you as his model, he will
soon be carrying the gospel throughout the world.
Truly, he is as you described him "a faithful and beloved brother." He has no desire to be set free in the
legal sense, but I must take the necessary steps to make
this possible so that he can move round the churches
with greater freeedom, for his testimony must be widely
heard.

From what Onesimus tells us of your plight and
health in Rome, we worry greatly about you and you
are constantly in our prayers. However, we have faith
that God who has brought you safely through so many
trials and dangers will preserve you and return you
to us soon. As you requested, our guest room awaits
you, together with a royal welcome from all your friends
at Colossae.

> Your grateful friend,
> Philemon

There Are Stormy Times Ahead

> *You must realize that in the last days the times will
> be full of danger. Men will become utterly self-centered,*

*greedy for money, full of big words. They will be proud
and contemptuous, without any regard for what their
parents taught them. They will be utterly lacking in
gratitude, purity, and normal human affections. They
will be men of unscrupulous speech and have no control over themselves. They will be passionate and unprincipled, treacherous, self-willed, and conceited, loving all the time what gives them pleasure instead of
loving God. They will maintain a façade of "religion,"
but their conduct will deny its validity. You must keep
clear of people like this. Their minds are distorted, and
they are traitors to the faith.*

*But you have known intimately both what I have
taught and how I have lived. Persecution is inevitable
for those determined to live really Christian lives, while
wicked and deceitful men will go from bad to worse,
deluding others and deluding themselves.*

*Yet you must go on steadily in those things that you
have learned and which you know are true. Remember
from what sort of people your knowledge has come and
how from early childhood your mind has been familiar
with the holy Scriptures, which can open the mind to
the salvation which comes through believing in Christ
Jesus. The Scriptures are the comprehensive equipment
of the man of God.*

Paul rounds off his discussion of the Day of the Lord
with a reassurance to all Christians who have suffered
persecution and calumny that God's judgment is working
itself out through their suffering. He is writing again to
the Thessalonians:

This Is How I Visualize the Last Judgment

*Without doubt [God] intends to use your suffering
to make you worthy of his Kingdom, yet his justice*

*will one day repay trouble to those who have troubled
you, and peace to all of us who, like you, have suffered.
This judgment will issue eventually in the terrific
denouncement of Christ's personal coming from Heaven
with the angels of his power. It will bring full justice
in dazzling flame upon those who have refused to know
God or to obey the gospel of our Lord Jesus Christ.
Their punishment will be eternal exclusion from the
radiance of the face of the Lord, and the glorious
majesty of his power. But to those whom he has made
holy his coming will mean splendor unimaginable. It
will be a breath-taking wonder to all who believe—
including you, for you have believed the message that
we have given you.*

*In view of this great prospect, we pray for you con-
stantly, that God will think you worthy of this calling,
and that he will effect in you all that his goodness
desires to do, and that your faith makes possible. We
pray that the name of our Lord Jesus Christ may become more glorious through you, and that you may
share something of his glory—all through the grace
of our God and Jesus Christ the Lord.*

The symbolism may owe something to apocalyptic
Jewish teaching, still deeply rooted in Paul's psychology,
but it is undoubtedly suffused with Christian hope. And
the message is unmistakable and needs no spelling out!

2

The Perennial Issue—Christianity and Politics

As the years wore on, the Day of the Lord did not dawn, and so the early Christian communities were faced with all the problems of living in a social order dominated by the Roman Empire. In other words, they became embroiled in politics.

The Roman Immigration Office to Paul

It has come to our attention that though you were born of Jewish parentage, you claim Roman citizenship by virtue of the fact your father was made a freedman by an eminent Roman official. You have also, on several occasions, used this status to challenge the jurisdiction over you of colonial courts.

We are, therefore, writing to inform you that under a new Immigration Act (Cap. CXXI—Laws of the Senate Consultum) a citizen of Rome and Colonies is no longer automatically entitled to citizenship of Imperial Rome. This restriction placed on nonpatrials has become necessary because of problems of over-population, housing, and work opportunities. Should you wish to be considered for full Roman citizenship, please fill in the enclosed application forms in triplicate. Until such time as your citizenship status has been finally determined you are hereby instructed to refrain from using your subordinate status as a citizen of Rome and Colonies for any official purposes.

Your Obedient Servant,
Enoch
Chief Immigration Officer

Paul had indeed used his Roman citizenship to get him out of the odd, tight corner, as at Philippi, and he had also claimed to be a true Hebrew to command the respect of Jewish Christians. But as his theology developed, he began to see the crux of the issue in theological rather than legalistic terms. Accordingly he replied to the Chief Immigration Officer, claiming a quite novel form of citizenship—novel in the sense that the country concerned existed on no known map. He made his point by quoting not only from his own writings but also those of his fellow apostle, Peter, and the probable author of the Letter to the Hebrews, Apollos:

The Nature of Christian Citizenship

We are citizens of Heaven; our outlook goes beyond this world. You are no longer outsiders or aliens, but fellow citizens with every other Christian—you belong now to the household of God. We have no permanent city here on earth, we are looking for one in the world to come. We live in this world only as strangers and

*temporary residents. You are God's "chosen genera-
tion," his "royal priesthood," his "holy nation," his
"peculiar people"—all the old titles of God's people
now belong to you.*

The reply of the Chief Immigration Officer was sharp
and to the point:

> It is my duty to remind you that Rome recognizes no God
> but Caesar, and that the "titles" to which you refer are asso-
> ciated with the Jewish nationalism that from time to time has
> attempted to undermine the peace and order of the Roman
> Empire. The penalty for subversion is death. Be warned!

In fact, Paul, in contrast to the fiery denunciations of
the Roman Empire by the writer of the Christian apocalyptic work we know as the book of Revelation and by
movements such as that of the Zealots, did not merely
recognize the state as a fact of life which the Christian
communities would have to learn to get along with. For
him, the state, any state, was an ordinance of God to preserve justice, order, and public morality. Obviously he
drew the line at Caesar-worship, but in other respects he
was a genuine political conservative whose position was
derived, not from expediency, but from carefully thought-
out convictions.

Governments, Even That of Rome, Are Made in Heaven

*Every Christian ought to obey the civil authorities,
for all legitimate authority is derived from God's
authority, and the existing authority is appointed under
God. To oppose authority then is to oppose God, and
such opposition is bound to be punished.*

*The honest citizen has no need to fear the keepers
of law and order, but the dishonest man will always
be nervous of them. If you want to avoid this anxiety,*

just lead a law-abiding life, and all that can come your way is a word of approval. But if you are leading a wicked life you have reason to be alarmed. The "power of the law" which is vested in every legitimate officer is no empty phrase. He is, in fact, divinely appointed to inflict God's punishment upon evil-doers.

You should, therefore, obey the authorities, not simply because it is the safest, but because it is the right thing to do. It is right, too, for you to pay taxes for the civil authorities are appointed by God for the good purposes of public order and well-being. Give everyone his legitimate due, whether it be rates, or taxes, or reverence, or respect!

Had Paul been writing five years later, following the disastrous fire in Rome for which Christians were made scapegoats, he might not have been so positive and un-critical in his endorsement of the state. At it was, he got a mixed reaction to his exposition of the role of government:

Paul from Augustus

My dear fellow,

What a splendid letter that was you sent to the church in Rome the other week; I found it difficult not to stand up and cheer. There's been much too much of this business of the church interfering in matters which don't concern it of late. Leave the politics to the senators, and let us Christians get on with our job of preaching Christ, praying, and so forth, that's what I say. I don't mind telling you I have made myself pretty unpopular in certain circles in the Roman Church. Being an ex-military man, I've felt there's been too much disrespectful if not revolutionary, talk among some of the young Christians. By heaven! A spell in the Legions would do them a world of good! You can imagine that for a man in my position to become a Christian at all has meant considerable social sacrifices. Some of my fellow officers cut me dead in the street, and I'm not even invited to my old regimental reunions any more. It hurts, old buddy. It hurts. I'm not complaining, mind you. We all have to make sacrifices for what we believe. But to have to put up with inflammatory sermons attacking my former comrades is just too much. Still, I think you've put these insubordinate elements well and truly in their place. Well done! I must say that for a Jew you're a real white man!

> Your comrade in arms,
> Augustus Gallius
> General (Rtd.), 3rd Legion

P.S. I enclose a copy of my pamphlet "Render unto Caesar . . . and unto God." Rather a good title I thought! You will note the similarities to your own argument.

A.G.

Predictably, Paul's defense of the state got a very different reception from some Jewish elements in the Church, and also from non-Christian Jews, some of whom had rebelled against the Roman authorities under the leadership of Crestus ten years before. The Emperor Claudius cleared the Jewish quarter of the city, but Jews had drifted back, among them members of the Zealot movement who were understandably incensed by Paul's letter:

The League of Young Zealots to Paul

How much longer must we live with the iron boot of Rome on our necks? We are the children of Moses who led our people from captivity to freedom. We will *not* pay taxes or go through the motions of showing respect to the Roman authorities. You boast of being a Jew converted to the way of the Nazarene and you encourage Roman Christians to behave like sheep. Have you forgotten that it was an alliance of Roman tyrants and Jewish puppets who executed the Nazarene? Obviously, your Roman citizenship means more to you than your Jewish blood. God made a convenant with our people, and we will not rest until our holy city, Jerusalem, is rid of Roman oppressors and we are free to worship the God of Abraham, Isaac, and Jacob without the permission of the Romans. Already, our leader, John of Gischala, has established a foothold in Jerusalem, and when the call comes, we in Rome will follow the example of Crestus and fight for our freedom even though we die in the attempt. In that struggle there can be no neutrals. And Christians will have to decide whether to carry the sword of God or Satan. We know enough about you and your adventures to be sure you are no coward. We are asking you to tell the Christians throughout the Empire to support our case. At present there is an uneasy truce between your religion and that of Caesar. But it cannot continue for long. Then will come your turn to go through the fire. Surely it is more pleasing to God to die for him than bow the knee to pagan gods?

The Sons of Crestus

There is no record of Paul engaging in open debate with Jewish nationalists, though he did preach that the state was a "restraining power" against anti-Christ, whose dominant characteristic he saw as anarchy and total confusion. It must be remembered that it was the military power and administrative genius of the Romans which enabled him to travel to the extremities of the known world preaching the gospel. No doubt he sent the Zealots

need for order

a copy of his letter to at least one Christian community making this point. It is unlikely that the young nationalists were impressed:

It's the State's Job to Keep Anti-Christ at Bay

You will probably also remember how I used to talk about a "restraining power" which would operate until the time "this Man," i.e. the Lawless Man, should come for the emergence of Anti-Christ. *Evil is already insidiously at work, but its activities are restricted until what I have called the "restraining power" is removed. When that happens the Lawless Man will be plainly seen—though the truth of the Lord Jesus spells his doom, and the radiance of the coming of the Lord Jesus will be his utter destruction.*

Paul's apparent lack of sympathy for the cause of Jewish nationalism cannot be taken to imply a pacifist attitude to war as such. Consider these words of counsel about Christian behavior:

The Strategy of Forgiveness

As for those who try to make your life a misery, bless them. Don't curse, bless. Don't pay back a bad turn by a bad turn, to anyone. *Never take vengeance into your own hands, my dear friends: stand back and let God punish if he will. For it is written:*
Vengeance belongeth unto Me: I will recompense.
And these are God's words:
If your enemy hunger, feed him;
If he is thirsty, give him to drink:
For in so doing thou shalt heap coals of fire upon his head.

*Don't allow yourself to be overpowered by evil. Take
the offensive—overpower evil by good!*

That statement seems to rule out of court any support
for the Zealots and to challenge any idea of a just revolution. It is not likely that such a concept had ever entered
Paul's mind, for who had ever known a *successful* rebel-
lion against the Roman Empire? What Paul seems to be
doing is not so much putting the case against Christians
taking up arms under any circumstances—that is an issue
which must be decided on grounds other than the appeal
to isolated texts from the Bible—as drawing up a kind of
first-century Geneva Convention. Obviously an enemy
who is hungry and thirsty is in a bad way, and more
likely to be a prisoner of war than an armed aggressor.
But he is certainly raising a crucial issue which must have
preoccupied not only potential revolutionaries but also
scholars as well:

Karlus Barthius to Paul

Meine gnädige Professor,
    Please to forgive meine terriblische sprachen du
language. Ich der studien der Romerbrief for to schrei-
ben dur very difficult unt very lange Buch. Ich finden
Ihr Romerbrief verry interestingk concerningk der Staat
under die Revolution. Please to comment auf meine
mathematikische formula unber die Staat unt die Revolution. Iche asken der expert in Paulische language
verlegen dis thesis; "Let the existing order—State,
Church, Law, Society, etc., in their totality be: (a b c d).
Let their dissolution by the Primal Order of God, by
which their totality is contradicted, be expressed by a
minus sign outside the bracket: $x - (a+b+c+d)$. It
is then clear that no revolution, however radical, which
takes place within the realm of history, can ever be

identical with the divine minus sign outside the bracket, by which the total of human ordinances is dissolved. Revolution can do no more than change the plus sign within the bracket—the plus, that is to say, which existing ordinances possess within the bracket because they exist—into a minus sign. The result of a successful revolution is therefore: $-$ $(-a-b-c-d)$. And now we see that for the first time the great divine minus sign outside the bracket has transformed the anticipatory, revolutionary minus sign into a genuine plus sign . . ." [1]
Du bis getten meine point, der gnädige Doktor?

Felicitations und Respect,
(Prof.) Karlus Barthius

To which Paul replied, as he often did:

The Peace of God preserve your mind!

Paul recognized the danger of becoming a "cult-figure" and so decided to warn the early Christians against "intellectuals" who would turn the gospel of Jesus into a complicated theological system. Had he read the completed work of Professor Karlus Barthius, would he have absolved *him* from any such charge?

Beware of Theologians!

I write like this to prevent you from being led astray by someone or other's attractive arguments. Be careful that nobody spoils your faith, through intellectualism or high-sounding nonsense. Such stuff is at best founded on men's ideas of the nature of the world and disregards Christ! For it is in him, *and in him alone, that men will find all the treasures of wisdom and knowledge.*
It is written:

[1]Barth, The *Epistle to Romans,* pp. 482-83, Oxford, 1953.

I will destroy the wisdom of the wise,
And the prudence of the prudent will I reject. For
consider, what have the philosopher, the writer, and
the critic of this world to show for all their wisdom?
Has not God made the wisdom of this world look
foolish? For it was after the world in its wisdom had
failed to know God, that he in his Wisdom chose to
save all who would believe by the "simple-mindedness"
of the gospel message.

It was in the everyday lives of Christians, rather than at the level of theological debate, that Paul's doctrine of the state was hard to live up to. From one side, Christians were attacked by Judaists; on the other side, they had neither the glory of martyrdom nor freedom to proclaim the gospel openly, but lived in a gray half-world. Little wonder the tension was hard to bear:

Paul from a Christian Mother

Dear Paul,

I hold no important position in the church here. I am just a mother trying to bring up her family as Christians and finding it harder every day. You know how we live. We do not suffer open persecution, yet we are treated as outcasts. The family who live next door attend the synagogue regularly and claim we are traitors to the true faith. The family on the other side are Romans who scorn us as traitors to the state. So we may as well be marooned on a desert island. My children have no one to play with; my husband can't get a job. Anonymous letters are pushed through our door frequently, accusing us of the vilest things. It has even been said that our Eucharist is a sex orgy, celebrated in the dark, with an infant child butchered on the altar and its flesh and blood eaten. Because we Christians address each other as "brother" and "sister," even this is used against us as evidence of some kind of vice ring.

I never expected it to be easy when our family was baptized as Christians. But I must confess that I find your instructions to obey the authorities willingly as agents of God impossible to reconcile with the constant insults of the legionaries or the bias of the magistrates who will never take a Christian's word against that of a Roman, no matter how many witnesses he can produce. Hardest of all to bear is the fact that things just drag on. Nothing happens to give us hope that Jesus will reign as king openly in Rome and that Caesar will be overthrown. Indeed, from what you say about the "powers that be" being appointed by God, I'm not even sure any more that this is what we ought to hope for.

I am truly sorry to burden you with my troubles. But my husband just seems to have lost faith, shrugs his shoulders, and says things will be all right in the end. But will they?

> Forgive me,
> Miriam

A Word of Cheer for Depressed Christians

In my opinion whatever we may have to go through now is less than nothing compared with the magnificent future God has planned for us. The whole creation is on tiptoe to see the wonderful sight of the sons of God coming into their own. The world of creation cannot as yet see reality, not because it chooses to be blind, but because in God's purpose it has been so limited—yet it has been given hope. And the hope is that in the end the whole of created life will be rescued from the tyranny of change and decay, and have its share in that magnificent liberty which can only belong to the children of God!

It is plain to anyone with eyes to see that at the present time all created life groans in a sort of universal travail. And it is plain, too, that we who have a foretaste of the Spirit are in a state of painful tension, while we wait for that redemption of our bodies will mean that at last we have realized our full sonship in him. We were saved by this hope, but in our moments of impatience let us remember that hope always means waiting for something that we haven't yet got. But if we hope for something we cannot see, then we must settle down to wait for it in patience.

Does Paul's great vision of the transformation of creation really answer Miriam's question and that of all ordinary Christians who have to put up with living in a hostile or indifferent society and see little to give them encouragement? Paul was an iron man with a cosmic vision. He painted on a large canvas and suffered on a heroic scale. God's lesser apostles who see only "more of the same" stretching ahead of them might be forgiven for feeling that Paul set standards beyond their reach. But he was unrelenting; supremely confident that Christian fidelity in small things was the quality which transmitted the hidden but active power of the Risen Christ into every nook and cranny of the old creation, imperceptibly changing it. And he was aware that his ragtag and bobtail army of followers numbered few who were people of secular importance:

God's Aristocrats

For look at your own calling as Christians, my brothers. You don't see among you many of the wise (according to this world's judgment) nor many of the ruling class, nor many from the noblest families. But God has chosen what the world calls foolish to shame the wise;

he has chosen what the world calls weak to shame the
strong. He has chosen things of little strength and small
repute, yes and even things which have no real existence
to explode the pretensions of the things that are—that
no man may boast in the presence of God.

He puts in two sentences the essence of Christian behavior which is universally relevant, including the two
extreme possibilities—being burned to death or bored to
death for Jesus' sake:

*Be on your guard, stand firm in the faith, live like
men, be strong! Let everything that you do be done in
love.*

Paul may have argued that the Roman magistrates were
servants of God for the punishment of wrongdoers, but he
took a dim view of Christians taking their disputes with
fellow Christians to court. This idea that pagans ought
not to be allowed to settle quarrels among the faithful
was a deeply held Jewish belief: so much so that according to the final chapter of the Acts of the Apostles, Paul
felt impelled to apologize to the church at Rome for
appealing to the Emperor when he was arrested in Jerusalem. But the Corinthian Christians were a litigious lot:

Cicilia to Paul

My dear Paul,
    I am writing to ask if you would be prepared to act as
a character witness in a slander suit I am bringing
against Paula, Pricilla, and two other members of our
Women's Circle. At our meeting last week, they had
the impertinence to demand my resignation from the
office of Treasurer, which I have held for a very long
time, on the grounds that I have been embezzling funds.

They didn't *actually* say that, of course. They are much too sly to come out into the open, but they claimed that our Annual Outing money was short. As you know, or probably you don't, because in spite of our repeated invitations you've not yet found time to spend a day with us at Cenchreae—a lovely spot we go to every year —I organize this trip and naturally deal with the financial arrangements. Ordinarily, I would treat their bitchy remarks with the contempt they deserve, but they've gone too far this time. Just because my husband's transport firm takes them there and my sister happens to own the cafe where we have our tea, you'd think they'd be grateful for the special terms I manage to obtain. But no, they as good as said I was running some family racket. And there's my dear husband, who doesn't enjoy the best of health, battling against labor trouble, etc., to see that they aren't disappointed even if he has to do the driving himself, and my sister whose cooking is renowned for miles around, though obviously with shortages and things, she isn't always able to provide the menu they ask for. But she does her very best.

I've known for some time that Paula and her gang have been trying to oust me from this office, but with Christian forbearance I've forgiven them for voting against me at the Annual Meeting three times running. But now they say that my financial report doesn't tally with what they reckon to have paid. It's nonsense, of course. I know how much there was in the urn I keep under my bed for safety. It's just that Nero—he's our dog—ate some of the parchment with the record of payments on it. Now, is my long service to this church to be rewarded with vicious allegations, just because of one of Nero's endearing little tricks? What I say is that God loves little doggies too—probably a lot more than these evil-minded so-called Christians.

At any rate, I'm taking the whole matter to court,

and my lawyer, who is my cousin (I suppose they'll try to make something of *that,* too!) feels that it would strengthen my case if I had as a character witness someone of standing in the Church. There's no problem getting you here for the hearing, my father, who owns Corinth's best shipping line (you've probably seen his ads—BOAZ Takes Good Care of You!) will be happy to provide you with a complimentary ticket.

Yours expectantly,
Cicilia

Of quarreling there seemed to be no end at Corinth.

Joshua Ben-Abel to Paul

Dear Sir,

This is to inform you that I have severed my connection with the church at Corinth and furthermore intend to take proceedings to recover a loan I made to the Church Council for a new Meeting House. Certain Jewish elements in the church—my own people!—claim to have evidence that because I was born in Rome I am an *uncircumcised* Jewish Christian! No better than a Gentile, in fact. I am treated like a second-class citizen. Well, they'll all get a shock when I produce evidence to the contrary in court because I intend to settle that matter as well as recover my money.

Joshua Ben-Abel

Tertius, a Slave, to Paul

Father,

I cannot write. This letter comes to you from prison, written for me by a fellow-prisoner who is a man of education. I am ashamed of what I have done, but also I do not understand why I am here. My story is this. A year ago the Christians gathered to celebrate a Love Feast in the way we have been taught. Because my master had kept me working for many hours in his garden, I was late for the Love Feast. Now the custom is that we all bring what food and drink we can and then share it. We poor cannot take much, if anything, while the rich members gather early and have a sumptuous meal before the service begins. Well, on this occasion I was very hungry and seeing a chicken in a basket I took it and ate it. It belonged to one of the wealthy members who had me arrested for theft, and so here I am. Am I mistaken in believing that your teaching is that we should share and share alike, with the rich helping the poor?

Master,
I am Tertius

For God's Sake Keep Away from the Courts!

When any of you has a grievance against another, aren't you ashamed to bring the matter to be settled before a pagan court instead of before the Church? Don't you know that Christians will one day judge the world? And if you are to judge the world do you consider yourselves incapable of settling such infinitely smaller matters? Are you really unable to find among your number one man with enough sense to decide a dispute between one and another of you, or must one brother resort to the law against another and that before those who have no faith in Christ! It is surely obvious that something must be seriously wrong in your church for you to be having lawsuits at all. Why not let yourself be wronged or cheated? For when you go to law against your brother you yourself do him wrong, for you cheat him of Christian love and forgiveness.

But in giving you the following rules, I cannot commend your conduct, for it seems that your church meetings do you more harm than good! For first, when you meet for worship I hear that you split up into small groups, and I think there must be truth in what I hear. It follows, then, that when you are assembled in one place you do not eat the Lord's *Supper. For everyone else tries to grab his food before anyone else, with the result that one goes hungry and another has too much to drink!*

Am I to commend this sort of conduct? Most certainly not!

There must have been those in Corinth and elsewhere who were impressed by Paul's qualities of leadership, mental ability, and oratorical power. It wouldn't have been surprising if they felt he might be an asset to some cause or other they were promoting:

From the Secretary of the Corinth Reform Party to Paul

Dear Sir,

Last evening we had a constituency meeting to choose a candidate for the forthcoming elections to the Senate. Your name was put before us as a man of reforming zeal. Several of our members had heard of your speech in Athens at the Areopagus, so you obviously have oratorical gifts as well. We feel that Corinth must be cleaned up. It is a sewer of corruption and iniquity and requires a powerful voice in the Senate to bring Rome's attention to our city's need for better law enforcement, improved communications, and so on. In our view, you would not only serve our people well but also adorn the Senate by your great gifts. As you know it has among its members some of the greatest philosophers, writers, and debaters of our time.

There is one matter I feel I ought to report. While our party could support much of your preaching and teaching, there is one issue which we consider might alienate some of our Jewish and Greek voters. This is your constant emphasis upon the crucifixion of the Nazarene—a controversial issue, I'm sure you would agree. A pledge from you that this subject would be well left alone in your election addresses, etc., is all we require. Obviously we have no desire to interfere with your private beliefs. We just don't want potential supporters driven away. Our motto has always been "Keep Religion out of Politics!" I hope for an early and favorable reply.

> Your future comrade in arms,
> Zenas
> Honorary Secretary,
> Corinthian Reform Party

Keep Quiet About the Cross? Never!

When I came to proclaim to you God's secret purpose, I did not come equipped with any brilliance of speech or intellect. You may as well know now that it was my secret determination to concentrate entirely on Jesus Christ himself and the fact of his death upon the Cross.

It is written:
I will destroy the wisdom of the wise,
And the prudence of the prudent will I reject.
What have the philosopher, the writer, and the critic of this world to show for all their wisdom? Has not God made the wisdom of this world look foolish? For it was after the world in its wisdom had failed to know God, that he in his Wisdom chose to save all who would

believe by the "simple-mindedness" of the gospel message. For the Jews ask for miraculous proofs and the Greeks an intellectual panacea, but all we preach is Christ crucified—a stumbling-block to the Jews and sheer nonsense to the Gentiles, but for those who are called, whether Jews or Greeks, Christ the power of God and the wisdom of God.

The Kingdom of God is not a matter of a flood of words but of the power of Christian living.

I don't write these things merely to make you feel uncomfortable but that you may realize facts . . .

Zenas, Again, to Paul

My dear Paul,

Our Party branch was very disappointed to receive your reply. If I may say so, you seem unaware that we count among our staunchest supporters some of the most influential and wealthy citizens of Corinth, a number of whom are, in fact, Christians. Don't you feel you are making too much of this Cross business? After all, your background is ideal for politics—a good school, Roman citizenship, etc. Why not take your rightful place in society? These eccentricities of yours are, if you will forgive me for saying so, making you look foolish in the eyes of powerful people who are in a position to further your career—not, I hasten to add, as an evangelist, or whatever you call yourself, but as a public personality with standing and respect, not only in the community at large but among highly placed Christians as well.

Won't you think again?

Hopefully,
Zenas

We Christian Outcasts Won't Impress the "Right" People

I think God means us, the special messengers, to appear last in the procession of mankind, like the men who are to die in the arena. For indeed we are made a public spectacle before the angels of Heaven and the eyes of men. We are looked upon as fools, for Christ's sake. We are considered weak, but you have become strong: you have found honor, we little but contempt. Up to this very hour we are hungry and thirsty, ill-clad, knocked about, and practically homeless. We still have to work for our living by manual labor. Men curse us, but we return a blessing: they make our lives miserable, but we take it patiently. They ruin our reputations, but we go on trying to win them for God. We are the world's rubbish, the scum of the earth, yes, up to this very day.

I take no special pride in the fact that I preach the gospel. I feel compelled to do so; I should be utterly miserable if I failed to preach it.

Christian communities were springing up all over the place, so it was inevitable that the more tidy-minded leaders of the churches should try to get more uniformity of practice among them. In particular, they were concerned about interchurch relations and issues which transcended national frontiers.

The Committee of Ten to Paul

Our dear Paul,

We, leaders of the Christian communities in Judea, Antioch, Tyre, Salamis, Galatia, Corinth, Rome, Colossae, Philippi, and Thessalonica, have just ended a long and rather argumentative meeting in Rome. We have decided to try to win support for a sort of World

Council of Churches. It would have, of course, a General Secretary and a number of other officials who are experts in particular subjects. It would hold conferences, councils, committees, study groups, and consultations with a view to getting some common mind among the various Christian churches on matters of mutual concern. It is our desire that the Christian communities should present a common front on important issues of our day . . . Rome is proving somewhat difficult—Peter obviously thought himself some kind of Pope—but the rest of us feel that we ought to take seriously our responsibilities as world citizens, passing resolutions to be submitted to the Emperor, lobbying Senators, etc., etc. But we felt that before launching any such organization we ought to get your reactions. Should you be favorably disposed to this idea, we would be honored if you were to become first Life President. Your good offices could then be enlisted to persuade the various churches to provide the funds to pay the Secretariat.

We are, -

Yours fraternally,

The Committee of Ten

Some Random Thoughts on Christian Unity and Diversity

1. We all share a common experience

When you [Gentiles] suffered at the hands of your fellow countrymen you were sharing the experience of the Judaean Christian churches, who suffered persecution by the Jews.

2. But the Church is set apart from the rest of society

Don't link up with unbelievers and try to work with them. What common interest can there be between

*goodness and evil? How can light and darkness share
life together? How can there be harmony between Christ
and the devil? What business can a believer have with
an unbeliever? Wherefore*

*Come ye out from among them and be ye separate,
saith the Lord.*

*Let us prove our reverence for God by consecrating
ourselves to him completely.*

3. Intercession is any Church or Christian's civil duty

*From the bottom of my heart I long and pray to God
that Israel may be saved!*

*Always maintain the habit of prayer: be both alert
and thankful as you pray. Include us, please, in your
prayers, that God may open for us a door for the en-
trance of the gospel. Pray that we may talk freely of
the mystery of Christ, and that I may make that mystery
plain to men, which I know is my duty.*

*Supplications, prayers, intercessions, and thanksgivings
should be made on behalf of all men: for kings and
rulers in positions of responsibility, so that our common
life may be lived in peace and quiet, with a proper sense
of God and of our responsibility to him for what we do
with our lives.*

4. Christendom has no capital nor earthly king

*Let no one boast of men. Everything belongs to you!
Paul, Apollos, or Cephas; the world, life, death, the
present or the future, everything is yours! For you belong to Christ, and Christ belongs to God!*

*The foundation is laid already, and no one can lay
another, for it is Jesus Christ himself.*

5. Each Church everywhere has the same goal—God's Plan

[God's] Secret was hidden to past generations of mankind, but it has now, by the Spirit, been made plain to God's consecrated messengers and prophets. It is simply this: that the Gentiles, who were previously excluded from God's agreements, are to be equal partners in God's promise given by Christ through the gospel. [God has] given this grace, to enable me to make plain to all men the meaning of that secret which he who created everything in Christ has kept hidden from the Creation until now. The purpose is that all the angelic powers should now see the complex wisdom of God's plan being worked out through the Church, in conformity to that timeless purpose which he centered in Jesus, our Lord.

When I think of the greatness of this great plan I fall on my knees before God the Father (from whom all fatherhood, earthly or heavenly, derives its name).

6. Peter stated the ultimate principle of Church-State relations

We must obey God rather than men. We will not, under any conditions, give up speaking of things we have seen and heard.

7. Regarding national differences, note my words at Athens

God who made the world and all that is in it, being Lord of both Heaven and Earth, does not live in temples made by human hands, nor is he ministered to by human hands, as though he had need of anything— seeing that he is the one who gives to all men life and breath and everything else. From one forefather he has created every race of men to live over the face of the whole Earth. He has determined the times of their existence and the limits of their habitation, so that they might search for God, in the hope that they might feel for him and find him—yes, even though he is not far from any one of us. Indeed it is in him that we live and move and have our being.

8. Good luck in your venture—but about paying the secretariat?

The Lord has ordered that those who proclaim the gospel should receive their livelihood from those who accept the gospel.

3

Teething Troubles

The Christian Church began when a little band of followers of Jesus of Nazareth discovered that God, by
raising him from the dead, confirmed his startling claims
and powerful teaching. They waited to see whether one
further promise he had made would be kept—that his
Spirit would take up permanent residence among them.
Pentecost clinched the matter, so Christians began to prepare themselves to change the world by meeting regularly
to study the teachings of the apostles, share a common
meal and pray together.

Probably more than any other apostle, Paul realized
just how radically new Christianity really was. It wasn't
just a reformed Judaism but a world-embracing faith. He
made the claim, astonishing for a Pharisee, that the
Christian Church was the New Israel, the people of God.
The Old Israel had been given its chance and thrown it
away. It had rejected the Messiah.

Paul, aflame with missionary zeal to take the gospel to

the ends of the known earth, found himself embroiled in all kinds of quarrels and disputes about doctrines and church order. He could be, I suspect, a short-tempered man, and nothing infuriated him more than slick talkers who set themselves up as "extraspecial messengers," as he sarcastically labeled them. From time to time he felt driven to state his credentials as an apostle:

Pardon My Conceit, but I'm More Than a Match for My Critics!

Let me advise you not to look upon me as a fool. Yet if you do, then listen to what this "fool" has to boast about.

I have worked harder than any of them.

I have served more prison sentences!

I have been beaten times without number.

I have faced death again and again.

I have been beaten the regulation thirty-nine stripes by the Jews five times.

I have been beaten with rods three times.

I have been stoned once.

I have been shipwrecked three times.

I have been twenty-four hours in the open sea.

In my travels I have been in constant danger from rivers and floods, from bandits, from my own country- men, and from pagans. I have known exhaustion, pain, long vigils, hunger and thirst, doing without meals, cold, and lack of clothing.

In Damascus, the town governor, acting by King Aretas' order, had men out to arrest me. I escaped by climbing through a window and being let down the wall in a basket. That's the sort of dignified exit I can boast about.

The Secretary of the Corinth Church to Paul

My dear Paul,

Thank you for that graphic account of your missionary journeys. You really are the greatest! What a time you must have been through! When you next visit us, I'm sure the Chairman of our Men's Supper Club will be after you to give us a talk, and I can promise you a full house!

However, that's not the main point of my letter. I write to you as a brother in Christ, and I pray you won't take offence. I think you do an injustice to some of your fellow preachers by rather overdoing this personal heroism stuff. I know it's presumptuous of me, but these hair-raising accounts of your adventures seem to me to have two unfortunate consequences. Firstly, they make ordinary Christians such as myself feel utterly inadequate. We attend Communion regularly, give generously to the poor, and live blameless lives, but we don't hit the headlines. Does this make us second-class Christians? My other point is that at least these leaders you criticize so severely do keep the show going, and I don't know where we would be without them. For instance, you have now missed seven meetings of our Finance Committee without so much as a written apology for absence. Now *I* understand that it's not easy to post a letter to us when you are shipwrecked, and so on. But there are others who miss no opportunity to discredit you. And you do rather play into their hands, you know, with your somewhat erratic behavior.

Please don't misunderstand me. Your epic journeys with the gospel will, I'm certain, live for ever in the annals of the Church. But if you don't uphold the good order of the Church, how do we reply to those who say that Paul is a law unto himself and that if he doesn't stick to the rules, why should they?

Frankly, our Church is in such a mess that we really need you here to sort things out rather than hopping up and down the walls of Damascus in a basket. For heaven's sake, what kind of behavior is that for an apostle?

Please forgive my bluntness, but I've felt I ought to say these things to you for a while now. Do take them in the spirit they are meant.

> Yours in Christ,
> Crispin
> Secretary, Church Council

I Was Being Sarcastic, You Dear Idiots!

I have made a fool of myself in this "boasting" business, but you forced me to do it. If I am going to boast, let me boast of all the things I was not clever enough to dodge! Even so, it is proof that I speak by the power of Christ.

The Christ you have to deal with is not a weak person outside you, but a tremendous power inside you. He was "weak" enough to be crucified, yes, but he lives now by the power of God. I am weak as he was weak, but I am strong enough to deal with you for I share his life by the power of God.

It is yourselves that you should be testing, not me. You ought to know by this time that Christ is in you, unless you are not real Christians at all.

By the truth of Christ within me, no one shall stop me from being proud of independence. Does this mean that I do not love you? God knows it doesn't, but I am determined to maintain this boast, so as to cut the ground from under the feet of those who profess to be special messengers on the same terms as I am. Special messengers? They are counterfeits of the real thing, dis-

honest practitioners, "special messengers" only by their own appointment. Nor do their tactics surprise me when I consider how Satan himself masquerades as an angel of light.

Koloketh, the Preacher, to Paul:

My dear Paul,

Allow me to introduce myself: I am known to the Christians at Corinth as the Preacher—a title, I hasten to add in all modesty, which has been thrust upon me because God in his infinite wisdom has chosen to give me certain oratorical gifts—I just open my mouth and words pour forth. The glory belongs to God, but the crowds flock to hear me. Hallelujah! Praise the Lord! If I may quote from a recent issue of the *Corinth Chronicle:*

> Why are the crowds flocking down Cicero Street every Seventh Day? To watch the wrestling or lion-baiting in the Arena or to see the latest play at the Odeum? Not at all. They are packing the Christian Meeting House to hear the renowned orator, Koloketh, who has become one of the city's great attractions.
>
> A handsome figure of a man with flowing silver hair and a silvery tongue to match, Koloketh's magnificent voice sobs and pleads, then roars and thunders as he denounces the sexual license, piracy, and vice which have made Corinth (in his words) "The sewer-city of the Mediterranean; the rubbish heap of discarded humanity."
>
> Whether one agrees with him or not, Koloketh is a most impressive personality. And he is reputed to be immensely knowledgeable. As he confessed modestly to your reporter, he can recite by heart the book of Leviticus, the Psalms, and the name, size, destination, and time of sailing of every ship in the port.
>
> Truly the followers of Venus will have to pull up the

thongs of their sandals if they are not to lose the crowds
to this modern Cicero, this daring Demosthenes . . .

I merely include this extract in order to reassure you
that some of us whom you seem to despise are reaping
a rich harvest for the Lord. Surely our success is proof
that the Spirit is at work among us. It is not for a
comparative newcomer such as myself to offer advice to
an "apostle," but I do feel that you are a little hard on
the Christians at Corinth. They are frankly terrified by
the tone of your letters and belittle themselves as utterly
unworthy followers of Jesus. Now, I, being like yourself
a preacher of the word, understand your psychological
hang-ups. You can't help your somewhat insignificant
appearance and lack of oratorical power. With your im-
pediment, I think it a miracle you can face the people
in public at all. Nor ought you to worry that other
preachers, such as myself, draw much larger crowds. I
have had occasion to chastise some of the leaders of the
Christian community here for comparing unfavorably
your congregation drawing power with my own. And
when a well-known Christian said recently that though
your letters were impressive and moving, your presence
and preaching was "feeble," I was the first to spring to
your defense.

But if I may be permitted to give you a little advice:
offer a little more comfort and reassurance and a little
less angry condemnation. Then I'm sure you too will
have the satisfaction of addressing a packed meeting
house. For no one grieves more than myself at the rows
of empty seats, which must discourage you greatly when
you come to preach the Word. And should you feel that
our Christian influence is dwindling anywhere, I am
more than willing to bring my team of Corinth Cru-
saders to rally the masses.

> Your colleague and fellow evangelist,
> Koloketh

P.S. My motto is "Scourge the Pagans, Shame the Jews, Comfort the Christians." It works miracles!

P.P.S. You've probably noted that my name, "Koloketh," means "the Preacher" as in Ecclesiastes. Weren't my parents farsighted in giving me such a name, in view of my later development! Hallelujah again! Surely infallible proof that the Spirit is with me . . . though the glory is God's, of course.

It Isn't Oratory but God's Power That Makes Christians!

So-and-so considers himself to belong to Christ. All right; but let him reflect that we belong to Christ every bit as much as he. I don't want you to think of me merely as the man who writes you terrifying letters. I know my critics say, "His letters are impressive and moving but his actual presence is feeble and his speaking beneath contempt." Let them realize that we can be just as "impressive and moving" in person as they say we are in our letters.

Of course we shouldn't dare include ourselves in the same class as those who write their own testimonials, or even to compare ourselves with them! All they are doing, of course, is to measure themselves by their own standards or by comparison within their own circle, and that doesn't make for accurate estimation, you may be sure. No, we shall not make any wild claims, but simply judge ourselves by that line of duty which God has marked out for us, and that line includes our work on your behalf.

I am afraid that your minds may be seduced from a single-hearted devotion to [Christ] by the same subtle means that the serpent used towards Eve. For apparently you cheerfully accept a man who comes to you preaching a different Jesus from the one we told you about, and you readily receive a spirit and a gospel quite different from the ones you originally accepted. Yet I cannot believe I am in the least inferior to these extraspecial special messengers. Perhaps I am not a polished speaker, but I do know what I am talking about, and both what I am and what I say is pretty familiar to you.

He that glorieth let him glory in the Lord. It is not self-commendation that matters, it is winning the approval of God.

His "gifts unto men" were varied. Some he made special messengers, some prophets, some preachers of the gospel; to some he gave the power to guide and teach his people. His gifts were made that Christians might be properly equipped for their service, that the whole body might be built up until the time comes when, in the unity of common faith and common knowledge of the Son of God, we arrive at real maturity.

Corinth Church Council Secretary to Paul Again

My dear Paul,

When we heard that you would not be calling at Corinth on your way to Macedonia our Church Council was in an uproar. We had prepared a special welcome for you, complete with a church supper cooked by our ladies. We'd even invited His Worship the Mayor, who had put off an important social engagement to be present—granted, he's a doddering old fool who would have rambled on for hours—but that's not the point. We are trying hard to get ourselves established in the city as a respectable and respected body of people. Our choir has been practicing a cantata in your honor, composed by the choirmaster and entitled "Hail to Paul, the Fearless Apostle." All this, as well as the public meeting we had widely advertised. Luckily, Koloketh volunteered at short notice to take your place, so the crowds won't be disappointed.

But . . . why do you do it, Paul? I know we Corinthian Christians have caused you a lot of anxiety. And there was, of course, that particularly unfortunate incident where one of our members was cohabiting with his father's wife, and for which you rightly admonished us. But we really do try, most of us, to live Christian lives. We've expelled that notorious sinner—Satan can have him for all we care—but is this any reason for punishing the rest of us by cutting us from fellowship with you?

Though the anti-Paul faction is jubilant that you've cancelled your visit, the rest of us are sick at heart. I had hoped that this visit would clear the air once and for all. Now, we hear you aren't coming. It's all very discouraging.

Sadly yours,
Crispin

I Think It Best to Stay Away from Corinth

I declare before God that it was to avoid hurting you that I did not come to Corinth. For though I am not responsible for your faith—your standing in God is your own affair—yet I can add to your happiness. And I made up my mind that I would not pay you another painful visit. For what point is there in my depressing the very people who could give me such joy? The real purpose of my previous letter [about that horrible sin and your general moral license] was in fact to save myself from being saddened by those whom I might reasonably expect to bring me joy. I wrote to you in deep distress and out of a most unhappy heart (I don't mind telling you I shed tears over that letter), not, believe me, to cause you pain, but to show you how deep is my care for your welfare.

This is my advice now. If the behavior of a certain person has caused distress, it does not mean so much that he has injured me, but that to some extent (I do not wish to exaggerate), he has injured all of you. But now I think the punishment you have inflicted on him has been sufficient. Now is the time to offer him forgiveness and comfort, for it is possible for a man in his position to be completely overwhelmed by remorse. I ask you to show him plainly now that you love him. If you will forgive a certain person, rest assured that I forgive him too. Insofar as I had anything personally to forgive, I do forgive him, as before Christ. We don't want Satan to win any victory here, and well we know his methods!

Trusting you, and believing that you trusted us, our original plan was to pay you a visit first, and give you a double "treat." We meant to come here to Macedonia after first visiting you, and then to visit you again on leaving here. Because we had to change this plan, does it mean we are fickle? Are we then the men to say one thing and mean another?

Corinth Philharmonic Choirmaster to Paul

Dear Sir,

At a special meeting of our Choir Committee, I was asked to write to you, expressing our concern, and indeed anger, that after all our practicing of the new cantata from my pen "Hail to Paul, the Fearless Apostle," we now hear you are not visiting us after all.

I am told that you are not musically inclined and so may not appreciate just how much trouble goes into the composition and preparation for public performance of a new choral work.

We are at a loss to understand the reason for your sudden change of plan, but it is widely rumored throughout the Christian community that it has to do with a case of sexual misbehavior on the part of one of our members. Now really! This, after all, is Corinth, not some Galilean country village. Aphrodite, and now Venus, has been for years our national goddess—the goddess of love. You and I are men of the world. Love takes many strange forms. Isn't it utter naïveté to imagine that Corinth as a city is going to change its ways because a small Christian sect has established itself here? I must say that I think we would have more success if we showed a little more tolerance towards our local customs and concentrated on spiritual matters. We are getting a reputation as killjoys. We have already lost our best tenor and one of the sopranos because they were caught in a compromising position behind the Odeum after choir practice the other week. Don't imagine I'm trying to excuse such behavior. I merely think you are out of touch with modern thinking on such matters.

However, my main reason for writing is that the choir, after taking a vote of all its members, resolved that my cantata, originally entitled "Hail to Paul, the Fearless Apostle," should be renamed "Hail to Koloketh, the Great Preacher," and I was asked to inform you accordingly. I may say that I voted against the proposition, but to no avail. This is just one indication of the strong feeling in Corinth about what is felt to be your narrow-mindedness on sexual matters.

Yours in the love of music,
Thespus

A Fine Lot You Once Were Before Christ Claimed You!

Have you forgotten that the Kingdom of God will never belong to the wicked? Don't be under any illusion—neither the impure, the idolater, or the adulterer; neither the swindler, the drunkard, the foul-mouthed, or the rapacious shall have any share in the Kingdom of God. And such men, remember, were some of you! *But you have cleansed yourselves from all that, you have been made whole in spirit, you have been justified before God in the name of the Lord Jesus and in his very Spirit.*

On his little Christian communities, Paul, who often seems a lonely man—he was certainly a childless one—lavished a parental love. He anguished over them. To some he was a father, stern yet anxious; to others he was as gentle as a mother with an unweaned child. The human, even vulnerable Paul is easily lost in the great, lengthy theological discourses of the Epistles. Yet his tenderness shows through again and again:

Never Forget You Are My Much-Loved Family

Our attitude among you was one of tenderness, rather like that of a devoted nurse among her babies. You will remember how we dealt with each one of you personally, like a father with his own children, stimulating your faith and courage and giving you instruction. Since we have been physically separated from you, my brothers (though never for a moment separated in heart), we have longed all the more to see you. Yes I, Paul, have longed to come and see you more than once—but somehow Satan prevented our coming.

75

Yet who could take your place as our hope and joy and pride when Jesus comes? Who but you, as you will stand before him at his coming? Yes, you are indeed our pride and our joy!

You know how handicapped I was by illness when I first preached the gospel to you. You didn't shrink from me or let yourselves be revolted at the disease which was such a trial to me. No, you welcomed me as though I were an angel of God, or even as though I were Jesus Christ himself! What has happened to that fine spirit of yours? I guarantee that in those days you would, if you could, have plucked out your eyes and given them to me. Oh my dear children, I feel the pangs of child-birth all over again till Christ be formed within you, and how I long to be with you now!

Lydia to Paul

My dear Paul,

I am greatly concerned about your health and well-being. You punish your body mercilessly by your constant traveling and the physical danger to which you expose yourself. You are a sick man and you choose not to have any wife to look after you. There is nothing improper nor worldly about the love I bear for you. I just wonder how you cope with the loneliness and fatigue that becomes more evident all the time.

And we Christians don't help you much by our quarreling and failure to match up to your expectations of us. Is there no way in which we can lighten your burden? Forgive me for saying so, but I sometimes detect a self-sufficiency in you which is little short of pride. After all, you introduced us to the love of Christ and that must surely be a two-way business. He who loves as you have loved all your converts must be prepared to receive love in return. Are we not all inter-dependent—one family in Christ? You have done so much for us. It could be a sign of grace to allow us to do more for you in return. But who am I, a seller of dyed cloth, to lecture Paul in theology?

Please take care of yourself and never forget that though you can refuse many forms of help, you cannot stop us praying for you!

Ever yours,
Lydia

Really, I'm Well Blessed with Friends!

I thank God for you Christians at Philippi whenever I think of you. It is only natural that I should feel like this about you all, for during the time I was in prison as well as when I was out defending and demonstrating the power of the gospel we shared together the grace of God. God knows how much I long, with the deepest Christian love and affection, for your companionship.

Just think of those who've helped me and whom I love: Timothy—he has been a son to me. Titus has worked by my side. Priscilla and Aquila, they risked their lives for me, and the friends of Jesus who meet together in their home; Stephanas and his family—the first people to become friends of Jesus in Greece, as Epaenetus was the first in Asia; relatives of mine, Andronicus and Junia who have been in prison with me, and there's Herodion too; Apelles—he has been a brave man; Rufus, he has done fine work for Jesus (his father carried the cross for Jesus); his mother looked after me as if she were my mother too; Gaius—I used to stay with him; he took care of me; Erastus, the city treasurer; Stachys and Persis—both of whom I love very much; what a hard worker Persis is; Apollos—

brother of mine in the service of Jesus; I began the work at Corinth, he carried it on, but it was God who made his work and mine grow; Epaphroditus—brother of mine too, in the service of Christ; Philemon—leader of the friends of Jesus in Colossae; and Onesimus, once his slave and now a friend of Jesus and his friend too; Aristarchus—who is a prisoner here in Rome with me; Mark—cousin of Barnabas, and Jesus Justus; these are the only Jewish friends of Jesus who have helped me in telling the good news; then there's Luke, my doctor.

Now I have everything I want—in fact I am rich. Your generosity is like a lovely fragrance, a sacrifice that pleases the very heart of God.

Lydia, Again, to Paul

Paul!

You are as stubborn as a mule! You haven't answered my question. I'm well aware that you have friends all over the place. It is your health and the frantic pace at which you live which concerns me. You won't be able to get away with these escapades of yours indefinitely. Sooner or later, the Roman authorities will decide to put you out of the way once and for all. Why not stop while you are still ahead—as they say at chariot races! You can spend more time consolidating the work you have already begun. Quite apart from strengthening the Christian communities, it would also do something to improve your health!

Lydia

It's Useless Arguing with a Fanatic!

Now, concerning myself, I want you to know, my brothers, that what has happened to me has, in effect, turned out to the advantage of the gospel. For, first of all, my imprisonment means a personal witness for Christ before the palace guards, not to mention others who come and go. Then, it means that most of our brothers, somehow taking fresh heart in the Lord from the very fact that I am a prisoner for Christ's sake, and show more courage in boldly proclaiming the Word of God.

We know that to those who love God, who are called according to his plan, everything that happens fits into a pattern for good.

In face of all this, what is there left to say? If God is for us, who can be against us? He that did not hesitate to spare his own Son but gave him up for us all—can we not trust such a God to give us, with him, everything else that we can need?

That Lydia should have the temerity to berate Paul is evidence of the revolution in the role and status of women which Christianity brought to the ancient world—a change of attitude Jesus himself demonstrated in his dealing with them. It must be confessed however that Paul was guilty of a certain inconsistency in his rules regarding the role of women in the Church. In one of his early letters, that to the Galatians, he stated roundly:

All of you who were baptized "into" Christ have put on the family likeness of Christ. Gone is the distinction between Jew and Greek, slave and free man, male and female—you are all one in Christ Jesus!

Yet he told the Christians at Corinth:

Let women be silent in church; they are not to be allowed to speak. They must submit to this regulation, as the law itself instructs. If they have questions to ask they must ask their husbands at home, for there is something indecorous about a woman's speaking in church.

Prunella to Paul

Dear Paul,

You really are a hypocrite! I became a Christian after hearing of the life of Jesus, his teaching, and particularly his attitude towards the women who followed him. They seemed to understand him better than some of the so-called apostles. I know that's little short of blasphemy, but I think it is true.

I was greatly encouraged, too, when I read that you had told the Galatian Christians that there is no sex distinction among those who are "in Christ." Now I hear that you have ordered women to keep quiet in church. If they have any questions, they must wait until they get home and ask their husbands. That's rich! Most of the men in church sleep solidly through the sermon!

Furthermore, we women must observe that outdated oriental custom of veiling our faces. For heaven's sake, do you think we are still in the Dark Ages? This is A.D. 60! We women are denied equality in every other walk of life. It was our sincere belief that in the Christian community we would at least find one place which offered us human dignity and our rightful place as the partners of men, and not their unquestioning and groveling servants. Oh, I know that women are given jobs to do in the Church such as caring for the sick and taking food to the poor. I even hear that there is actually a woman deacon, Phoebe, in Cenchreae. No doubt it's pure coincidence that she happens to be the wealthiest woman in the city!

Which is it to be, Paul? Are we truly part of a fellowship that knows no distinction between male and female, or is that just so much hot air?

Prunella

P.S. Since I have no husband, who do I ask to explain the sermon to me?

Here Is the Reasoning Behind My Instructions

Christ is the head of every individual man, just as a man is the "head" of the woman and God is the head of Christ. Thus it follows that if a man prays or preaches with his head covered, he is, symbolically, dishonoring him who is his real head. But in the case of a woman, if she prays or preaches with her head uncovered it is just as much a disgrace as if she had had it closely shaved. And if to be cropped or shaved is a sign of disgrace to women (as it is with many peoples), then that is all the more reason for her to cover her head.

A man ought not to cover his head, for he represents the very person and glory of God, while the woman reflects the person and glory of the man. For man does not exist because woman exists, but vice versa. Man was not created originally for the sake of woman, but woman was created for the sake of man. For this reason a woman ought to bear on her head an outward sign of man's authority for all the angels to see.

Prunella, Again, to Paul

Come off it, Paul! "Man does not exist because woman exists but vice versa"—when did you last hear of a man giving birth to anything other than half-baked ideas like that? I presume you had a mother. Do *you* exist because she existed or vice versa?

> Unconvinced,
> Prunella

You Are Taking Me Too Literally!

Of course, in the sight of God neither "man" nor "woman" has any separate existence. For if woman was made originally for man, no man is now born except by a woman, and both man and woman, like everything else, owe their existence to God. But use your own judgment, do you think it right and proper for a woman to pray to God bare-headed? Isn't there a natural principle here, that makes us feel that long hair is disgraceful to a man, but of glorious beauty to a woman? We feel this because the long hair is the cover provided by nature for the woman's head. But if anyone wants to be argumentative about it, I can only say that we and the Churches of God generally hold this ruling on the matter.

Prunella to Paul

Sorry, but I think it's the old Jew of Tarsus rather than the servant of Christ speaking. I'm not convinced, and I'm very disappointed in you.

> Goodbye,
> Prunella

Prunella was, of course, right. It *was* the Jew of Tarsus speaking. Paul had been brought up in this oriental city where women of good reputation always wore veils in public. As is the case of many parts of the Middle East to this day, the veil is a sign of a woman's dignity and honor. To appear in public without one was to invite at the very least insult, and possibly condemnation as a prostitute.

Paul was a man of his time. Today he would be called a literalist. He undoubtedly accepted the Genesis account of the creation which described how man was made first and woman as an afterthought to provide him with a helpmate and companion. Granted such a background, Paul probably felt that Christianity was revolutionary enough without affronting contemporary society by riding roughshod over customs regarding women which were of minor significance compared to the central theme of the Christian faith. What cannot be denied is that Paul held in high honor many women who were among the first Christians. And he was prepared to break his own rules when the Spirit overruled *him* and spoke through a woman in the assembly of Christians. His insistence that when the Spirit seized a woman no one had the right to silence her was clearly stated. He felt that such a prophetess ought to be veiled so that those gathered together would not be so outraged by her violation of long-standing custom that they were deaf to what she had to say.

None of this, of course, acquits Paul of the charge of inconsistency. But who are we to condemn? Almost two thousand years later, in whole sectors of the Church, we resist the claims of women to a genuine priestly vocation on the basis of arguments which even our medieval forebears might find barbaric, sordid, and totally irrational. To quote a Church of England Bishop, who had better remain nameless, in a pastoral letter arguing against the admission of women to the priesthood, "There are certain times when women are unclean, and should they be priests, they would defile the altar of God." That was 1971. In comparison, Paul was positively enlightened.

The church at Jerusalem, whose pillars were James, Peter, and John, directed its mission to Jews alone. Paul and Barnabas, however, were busy evangelizing non-Jews —a task which soon raised problems. Need Gentile Christians observe the Jewish law and undergo, for example, circumcision? Paul decided to visit Jerusalem and discuss the whole question of the relation between Jewish and Gentile versions of the gospel. As he explained to the Galatian Christians, who were, to put it mildly, confused about the issue:

Stop Fighting a Battle That's Already Been Won!

I went up to Jerusalem again, this time with Barnabas, and we took Titus with us. My visit on this occasion was by divine command, and I gave a full exposition of the gospel which I preach among the Gentiles. I did this first in private conference with the Church leaders, to make sure that what I had done and proposed doing was acceptable to them. Not one of them intimated that Titus, because he was a Greek, ought to be circumcised. As far as the leaders of the conference were concerned (I neither know nor care what their exact position was: God is not impressed with a man's office), they had nothing to add to my gospel. In fact they recognized that the gospel for the uncircumcised was as much my commission as that the gospel for the circumcised was Peter's. When, therefore, James, Cephas, and John saw how God had given me his grace, they held out to Barnabas and me the right hand of fellowship, in full agreement that our mission was to the Gentiles and theirs to the Jews. The only suggestion they made was that we should not forget the poor—and with this I was, of course, only too ready to agree.

So Paul and Barnabas went happily on their way under the impression that Gentiles need not be circumcised and that the only obligation laid on the non-Jewish daughter churches was to provide some financial support for the church at Jerusalem. But at Antioch, Paul found himself in dispute with Peter, who at first mixed happily with Gentile Christians to the extent of adopting their local customs, which included the ignoring of Jewish food laws. At the instigation of representatives of James, Peter stopped sharing a common meal with Gentiles, much to Paul's fury, which was not lessened by the fact that Barnabas began to share Peter's misgivings.

The reason for this radical change of policy was probably a circular letter drawn up by the more narrow-minded of the leaders of the church at Jerusalem and sent shortly after Paul's departure to some of the other churches. This letter became known as the Apostolic Decree and is to be found in Acts 15.

Doing the Dirt on Paul

We, the apostles and elders, send greetings to our brothers of Gentile origin in Antioch, Syria, and Cilicia. Forasmuch as we have heard that some of our number, without any instructions from us, have disturbed you with their talk and unsettled your minds, we have resolved unanimously to send our chosen representatives with our well-beloved Barnabas and Paul, who have devoted themselves to the cause of our Lord Jesus Christ. We are therefore sending Judas and Silas, who will themselves confirm this by word of mouth. It is the decision of the Holy Spirit, and our decision, to lay no further burden on you beyond these essentials: you are to abstain from meat that has been offered to idols, from blood, from anything that has been strangled, and from fornication. If you keep yourselves from these things you will be doing right.

Farewell.

The honeyed tones of this letter do not disguise the fact that the more narrow-minded of the church leaders in Jerusalem had gone back on their agreement with Paul. Aside from the shining insincerity of referring to Paul as "well-beloved" and putting a couple of Jewish "heavies" —Judas and Silas—on his tracks to check the orthodoxy of his teaching, they had imposed a further prohibition upon Gentile Christians. To ban the eating of meat that had been offered to idols might seem a trivial issue. At the time, however, it created serious practical difficulties in Gentile communities where the meat market was to be found in the neighborhood of some temple or other. So *all* meat, except that sold by a Jewish butcher who observed the *kosher* regulations, was potentially an offering to idols.

From Vesuvius to Paul

Dear Sir,

You may have heard of me. They call me "Vesuvius" here in Pompeii because I am a wrestler whose bellows of rage terrify my opponents and remind the crowd of the volcano which rumbles above our city. I am, so to speak, the only Christian wrestler in captivity—and this is my problem. To keep up my strength I need meat in big quantities, and here's the snag. My dear wife, who is also a Christian, will not go near the meat stalls which are set up just outside the chapel of the Caesar-cult because she says that if we eat food which has been consecrated to idols that means we are behaving as though these false gods exist. To me, that is just

Another variation of the same problem required Paul's advice:

Martius to Paul

My dear Paul,

I have followed with great interest the debate in Gentile churches about the Christian's right to eat meat offered to idols. My problem is slightly different. I live in a community most of whose citizens are members of the Orphic and Pythagorean sects. As you will know, they are strict vegetarians. We also have a small number of Essene Jews who follow the same practice. I could willingly accept your advice and eat meat with a clear conscience but for one thing. James, the brother of Jesus, bishop of the church at Jerusalem, has honored me with his friendship, and he is also a vegetarian. So I must ask myself, whom should I follow, Paul or James? He is of course a Jew, and I am a Gentile, but I am torn between my respect for him and my conviction that your advice is sound. And naturally, what applies to vegetarianism also raises the question of the keeping of holy days. James strictly observes the Sabbath, and others of his followers fast from time to time.

> Your comments, please.
> Perplexed,
> Martius

People Are Different, and Christ's Kingdom Has Room for All

The Kingdom of Heaven is not a matter of whether you get what you like to eat and drink, but of righteousness and peace and joy in the Holy Spirit. In view of this tremendous fact, don't worry about what you eat

or drink, or what holy days you ought to observe, or
bother about new moons or Sabbaths. All these things
have at most symbolical value: the solid fact is Christ.

Again, one man thinks some days of more importance
than others. Another man considers them all alike.
Let every one be definite in his own convictions. If a
man specially observes one particular day, he does so
"to God." The man who eats, eats "to God," for he
thanks God for the food. The man who fasts also does
it "to God," for he thanks God for the benefits of fast-
ing. Surely we shouldn't wish to undo God's work for
the sake of a plate of meat!

I freely admit that all food is, in itself, harmless, but
it can be harmful to the man who eats it with a guilty
conscience. We should be willing to be both vegetarians
and teetotallers if by doing otherwise we should impede
a brother's progress in the faith. Your personal convictions are a matter of faith between yourself and God,
and you are happy if you have no qualms about what
you allow yourself to eat. Yet if a man eats meat with
an uneasy conscience about it, you may be sure he is
wrong to do so. For his action does not spring from his
faith, and when we act apart from our faith we sin.

It is to God alone we have to answer for our actions.

4

How to Start a New Religion

Paul was a missionary and not a theologian. The distinction is important. The theologian must accept the impossible task of finding a neat and tidy way of describing God who is, by definition, unknowable—the object of faith rather than the subject of certain knowledge. The missionary does his thinking on the march, bursting through barriers of hostility and indifference on the tidal wave of the Spirit; facing and overcoming the challenge of other religions and none; dealing with a thousand and one practical problems as they arise; denied the leisure to write definite works of theology which confirm or reject the thinking of other theologians. Paul knew *what* he believed and *why* he believed it, but he was certainly no precise, consistent scholar. And this, not because he lacked the mental apparatus but because time was short, the hour was late, and thousands knew nothing of his Savior. The nitpickers of religion, the pernickety-minded systematizers, poised to pounce on Paul's slightest inconsistency, must have been a sore trial for him. It could have happened something like this:

Asyncritus to Paul

My dear Paul,

Thank you for your good wishes in your latest letter to Rome. I greatly value them as I respect you and your work. I wonder whether I might presume on your valuable time to get your ideas for a book I am writing on *Religions of Our Time?* Though I am heart and soul a follower of Jesus, I must try to be quite objective and relate the Christian faith to the other beliefs to be found here. So far I have dealt with the Athenian cult of the Mysteries of Eleusis with its emphasis upon the quest of the goddess Demeter for her daughter, lost in the underworld. In the same chapter I also analyze the cult of Dionysus and the Orphic mysteries. I have also studied the Egyptian religion of Isis and Osiris which, as you know, is gaining in popularity here in Rome.

I have a whole section on the spread from Asia Minor of the cult of Cybele, the Great Mother, and her husband, Attis. And of course I could not ignore what seems to me the noblest of all oriental cults, that of the Persian god, Mythra. Throw in Zoroaster, Caesar-worship, and Judaism, and you will see what a formidable task I have set myself!

For us Gentiles, you are naturally the supreme authority on Christ-worship, and I would be much obliged if you could give me some account of the way in which God has led you from Pharisaism to your present theological position. Sorry to give you this trouble, but you know us scholars—we are like a dog with a bone when it comes to getting at the truth!

Yours ever,
Asyncritus

Let Me Begin at the Beginning—with Facts, Not Theory

The gospel I preach to you is no human invention. No man gave it to me, no man taught it to me; it came to me as a direct revelation from Jesus Christ. For you have heard of my past career in the Jewish religion, how I persecuted the Church of God with fanatical zeal and, in fact, did my best to destroy it. I was ahead of most of my contemporaries in the Jewish religion, and had a greater enthusiasm for the old traditions. But when the time came for God (who was responsible both for my physical birth and for my being called by his grace), to reveal his Son within me so that I might proclaim him to the non-Jewish world, I did not, as might have been expected, talk over the matter with any human being. I did not even go to Jerusalem to meet those who were special messengers before me—no, I went away to Arabia and later came back to Damascus. It was not until three years later that I went up to Jerusalem to see Peter, and I only stayed with him just over a fortnight. I did not meet any of the other special messengers, except James, the Lord's brother.

Now, my brothers, I want to speak about the gospel which I have previously preached to you, which you accepted, in which you are at present standing: that Christ died for our sins, as the Scriptures said he would; that he was buried and rose again on the third day, again as the Scriptures foretold. He was seen by Cephas, then by the Twelve, and subsequently he was seen simultaneously by over five hundred Christians, of whom the majority are still alive, though some have since died. He was then seen by James, then by all the special messengers and last of all, as if to one born abnormally late, he appeared to me! I am the least of the special messengers, and indeed I do not deserve that title at all, because I persecuted the Church of God.

But what I am now I am by the grace of God. The rising of Christ from the dead is the very heart of our message.

Asyncritus to Paul

My dear Paul,

Thank you for your prompt reply and the brief autobiographical notes it contained. I wonder if I might press you further on one particular point? You claim that your gospel is "no human invention." But bearing in mind that we are all influenced by the intellectual and religious environment in which we live; that ideas are like the air we breathe—we take them in without necessarily being aware of their source—to what extent, if any, is your belief in the dying and rising of Jesus related to the myths of the Redeemer-Gods such as Adonis, Osiris, and Attis? As you know, adherents of these cults refer to their particular god as a "Lord" who died and was resurrected, opening the way of salvation to all who by their union with him shared his experience. Might some of these teachings have influenced yours and become part of your theology? I'm sure you don't need me to remind you of the controversy at Antioch, where converts from paganism interpreted the preaching of Christians there as worship of a cult-God, Jesus. Knowing the endless trouble this Hellenized Christian heresy has caused, you will understand why I am anxious to get absolutely clear the place of Christ in your thinking and teaching.

Sorry to be such a nuisance.

Yours ever,
Asyncritus

Paul could, and possibly did, remind Asyncritus that the use of the term "Lord" of Jesus was not confined to

Gentiles alone. As early as Pentecost, Peter, who could hardly be accused of being a Hellenist, declared that "God has made both Lord and Christ this Jesus whom you crucified." And in the closing sentences of his first Letter to Corinth, Paul uses an Aramaic phrase—*Maranatha*—which can mean "Our Lord is coming" or "May our Lord come"; but whatever its precise meaning, the phrase and its use in Communion services confirms that Palestinian as well as Gentile Christians affirmed the Lordship of Christ. Paul undoubtedly infuriated some Jewish Christians by his tendency to drive a coach and horses (or to be historically more accurate, a donkey and cart) through some aspects of the old faith. But nowhere does he comment that even his bitterest Jewish critics complained about his teachings concerning Jesus. On this, at least, the early Church was united. Christians every where were those who "called upon the name of the Lord." And in essence, to acknowledge the Lordship of Christ was not to be wafted away on clouds of weird spirituality or take part in the dark, secret rituals of the mystery religions; it was to enter a Kingdom. This Kingdom was partly a present possession, but in its fullness a future inheritance. But in both its present and future dimensions, that Kingdom was barred to those who engaged in the bizarre or depraved behavior associated with some of the other religions of the time:

Jesus Is Lord of a Kingdom, Not a Cult

We must never forget that he rescued us from the power of darkness, and reestablished us in the Kingdom of his beloved Son, that is, in the Kingdom of Light. For it is by his Son alone that we have been redeemed and have had our sins forgiven.

The Kingdom of Heaven is not a matter of a flood

of words but of the power of Christian living. Nor is it a matter of ritual eating and drinking but of righteousness, peace, and joy in the Holy Spirit.

Neither the immoral nor the dirty-minded nor the covetous man (which latter is, in effect, worshiping a false god) has any inheritance in the Kingdom of Christ and of God.

God has placed everything under the power of Christ and has set him up as head of everything for the Church. For the Church is his body, and in that body lives fully the one who fills the whole wide universe.

Asyncritus to Paul

Here's the pest again! I note that in your writings you often seem to use "Christ" and "God" interchangeably. I know that you are proud of the strict belief in one God of your Jewish forebears. Dare I presume on your time to answer for me this question: What relation is there between Jesus Christ the Lord and God the Father? Someone has suggested to me that you seem to believe in one God, and another divine being, Christ, who is nearly, but not quite God?

All Right—Let Me Try to Explain

God was in Christ personally reconciling the world to himself—not counting their sins against them—and has commissioned us with the message of reconciliation. We are now Christ's ambassadors.

We are Christ's and Christ is God's.

He, who had always been God by nature, did not cling to his prerogatives as God's equal, but stripped himself of all privilege by consenting to be slave by *nature and being born as mortal man. And, having become man, he humbled himself by living a life of utter obedience, even to the extent of dying,* and the death he died was the death of a common criminal. *That is why God has now lifted him so high, and has given him the name beyond all names, so that at the name of Jesus "every knee shall bow," whether in Heaven or earth or under the earth. And that is why, in the end, "every tongue shall confess" that Jesus Christ is the Lord, to the glory of God the Father.*

My constant endeavor is to present the Gentiles to God as an offering which he can accept, because they are sanctified by the Holy Spirit. And I think I have something to be proud of (through Christ, of course) in my work for God. I am not competent to speak of the work Christ has done through others, but I do know that through me he has secured the obedience of Gentiles in word and deed, working by sign and miracle and all the power of the Spirit.

Now Christ is the visible expression of the invisible God. He existed before creation began, for it was through him that everything was made. Through him, and for him, also, were created power and dominion, ownership and authority. In fact, every single thing was created through, and for, him. He is both the first principle and the upholding principle of the whole scheme of creation.

Paul was, of course, more concerned to preach Christ than to define him. For him, Christ was not a "problem" but the answer to the deepest needs of men. The theological questions which perplexed later generations of Christians didn't worry him. He succeeded in interpreting God in a Christian way; neither the stern lawgiver of his Jewish background nor the abstraction of Greek would satisfy the scholarly aspirations of Asyncritus; even more doubtful that Paul had any interest in doing so. He was much more anxious to assure Asyncritus that it was through the "grace of the Lord Jesus" that he would come to know "the love of God." Let the scholars argue. He had seen the glory of God in the face of Jesus Christ. For him that was the gospel about which there was no room for compromise; as some Christians in Galatia discovered when Paul heard they were reverting to the old Jewish law:

I Taught You "the" Gospel—and Don't You Forget It!

I am amazed that you have so quickly transferred your allegiance from him who called you in the grace of Christ to another "gospel"! Not, of course, that it is or ever could be another gospel, but there are obviously men who are upsetting your faith with a travesty of the gospel of Christ. Yet I say that if I, or an angel from heaven, were to preach to you any other gospel than the one you have heard, may he be damned! You have heard me say it before and now I put it down in black and white—may anybody who preaches any other gospel than the one you have already heard be a damned soul!

Professor J. Suetonius to Paul

Dear "Doctor" Paul!

I and a number of other scholars in this area are gravely concerned at the absolute statements you continue to make about what the gospel is and what is it not. You seem to have developed some grandeur delusion! To claim that anyone who interprets the gospel in any way other than your own is damned is, to put it mildly, insufferable arrogance. You are not the only apostle, you know: indeed, I myself am related on my wife's side to one of the *real* apostles, a man who knew Jesus personally during his earthly life. And I don't mind telling you that he was as shocked as the rest of us when we heard that you had the effrontery to give Peter—Peter himself!—a public dressing-down for eating at the same table as his people rather than with Gentiles.

I regard your teaching concerning the law to Christians at Galatia and elsewhere as either mischievous or plain ignorant. You have obviously never read my own standard work, harmonizing the teaching of Jesus with that of the oral traditions attached to Mosaic law. This book, I may say, was most favorably reviewed in the best journals. I trust you don't suggest that *I* am damned!

I think you should know that many of us in academic positions are very worried about your pernicious influence upon our students. Only the other day, a student had the impudence to stand up in the middle of my lecture and say that my exposition of the law in the light of modern scholarship was sub-Christian! And he quoted *you* as his authority! "If Christ is in you," he shouted, "you are free!" Free to do what? I may ask. Murder? Desecrate the Sabbath? Show disrespect for parents and elders? Is it any wonder that we are being engulfed by a tide of permissiveness that is turning Galatia into a second Gomorrah?

However, a number of prominent citizens have formed a committee, of which I have the honor to be chairman, dedicated to restoring the Mosaic law—interpreted, of course, in a truly Christian manner—to a central place in our society. So this letter is an earnest attempt to gain your cooperation in refraining from spreading irresponsible doctrines among our people—otherwise I can

promise you a hot time on the next occasion you show
your face in this district.

> Yours indignantly,
> J. Suetonius,
> Doctor of Sacred Law

Are You Trying to Put Christ Back on the Cross?

*I will ask you one simple question: did you receive
the Spirit of God by trying to keep the law or by believing the message of the gospel? Surely you can't be
so idiotic as to think that a man begins his spiritual life
in the Spirit and then completes it by reverting to outward observances? Does God, who gives you his Spirit
and works miracles among you, do these things because
you have obeyed the law or because you have believed
the gospel? Ask yourselves that.*

*While we were "children" we lived under the author-
ity of basic moral principles. But when the proper time
came God sent his Son, born of a human mother and
born under the jurisdiction of the law, that he might
redeem those who were under the authority of the law
and lead us into becoming, by adoption, true sons of
God. You, my brother, are not a servant any longer;
you are a son.*

*Those who belong to Christ have crucified their old
nature with all that it loved and lusted for. If our lives
are centered in the Spirit, let us be guided by the Spirit.*

*Let us not be ambitious for our own reputations, for
that only means making each other jealous.*

Professor Suetonius, Again, to Paul

Thank you so much for your sermon! It seems to me
that before you start lecturing your betters, you ought

to study the Scriptures more thoroughly. For example, I note that in a letter to the Christians at Corinth (who God knows need the disciplines of the law!) you refer to the fact that 23,000 Jews died of the plague in Shittim. If you look up the appropriate reference in the Pentateuch (Numbers 20:9) you will find that it was 24,000 Jews who perished. A small matter. But no one who is careless of matters of minor accuracy has the scholarship or authority to teach others the major truths of Scripture.

Perhaps you would care to enroll as an undergraduate here!

J. Suetonius

The professor was technically right (Paul *had* gotten the reference wrong), yet psychologically wrong. Paul's letters reveal an intimate knowledge of the Old Testament. In fact, he knew it so well that he could misquote it in the way we are prone to do when we rely on memory and don't bother to look up the actual text. But Paul had neither the time nor inclination to take part in a Bible quiz with a pedant like Suetonius. He had other major matters relating to the person of Jesus to clarify for the benefit of churches and individuals who made serious inquiries of him.

Benjamin, a Disciple of Philo, to Paul

Dear Paul,

I am a student and follower of our great Jewish thinker and theologian, Philo, who you will be sorry to hear is now so sick and frail that he is confined to his house in Alexandria. His enforced inactivity suits, I'm sure, his mystical temperament; you, with your active nature, constantly on the move, would find such a state unbearably trying! My master, as you know from reading his words, has spent his life trying to harmonize the Jewish Scriptures with Greek philosophy, and especially with the teaching of Plato, as well as Aristotle and the Stoics. I, in turn, am attempting to trace the impact of Philo's ideas upon other great thinkers of our time, of whom, if I may presume to say so, you are one.

I am particularly interested in that part of your teaching concerning Jesus as the "Heavenly Man." According to Philo, the Heavenly or Ideal Man is referred to in Genesis 1:27—"So God created Man in his own image"; the second man, the historic Adam who sinned and became the fleshly father of our race, is the man of Genesis 2:7, "So the Lord God formed a man from the dust of the ground and breathed into his nostrils the breath of life." Now, what I am anxious to know is whether your teaching of the preexistent Christ is derived from Philo's view regarding the Ideal or Heavenly Man.

You will understand how important it is for both Christians and the followers of Philo to make common cause against the flagrant paganism which has let loose a flood of degradation, immorality, and blasphemy upon our society. Possibly this doctrine may provide common ground on which cultured Judaists, Greek philosophers, and Gentiles who revere the teachings of Philo can stand together with your own followers and try to raise our fallen society to a higher level of nobility. Alexandrian Christians have already assured me of the high esteem in which they hold Philo.

I would greatly value your considered opinion on this matter.

Yours respectfully,
Benjamin of Alexandria

Sorry! for Me, Christ Is Unique

The Gospel is centered in God's Son, a descendant of David by human genealogy and marked out as the Son of God by the power of that Spirit of holiness which raised him to life again from the dead. What the law could never do God has done by sending his own Son in a form like that of our sinful nature.

The divine nature was his from the first; yet he did not think to snatch at equality with God, but made himself nothing, assuming the nature of a slave. Bearing the human likeness, revealed in human shape, he humbled himself, and in obedience accepted even death —death on a cross. Therefore God raised him to the heights and bestowed upon him the name above all names, that at the name of Jesus every knee should bow—in heaven, on earth, and in the depths—and every tongue confess, "Jesus is Lord," to the glory of God the Father.

Benjamin, Again . . .

Dear Paul,

Forgive my temerity. Who am I to argue with you, but is there not a contradiction in the explanation of the person of Christ you so kindly sent me? I may have misunderstood you, but sometimes you seem to be claiming that Christ was the eternal Son of God who at a certain point in time was sent into the world, at others that Christ was a man of Jewish ancestry who became God's Son by the fact of his Resurrection. Now I can understand how a being could be human but not pre-existent or preexistent and not human, but for the life of me I don't see how he could be *both*. I am puzzled but willing to be convinced.

Yours ever,
Benjamin

P.S. Possibly if you could explain the relationship between Christ and Adam as you see it, I might find it easier to compare your basic teaching with that of Philo.

Adam Ushered in the Old Age; Christ, the New Age

Adam, the first man, corresponds in some degree to the man who was to come. But the gift of God through Christ is a very different matter from the "account rendered" through the sin of Adam. For while as a result of one man's sin death by natural consequence became the common lot of men, it was by the generosity of God, the free giving of the grace of the one man Jesus Christ, that the love of God overflowed for the benefit of all men.

Nor is the effect of God's gift the same as the effect of that one man's sin. For in the one case one man's sin brought its inevitable judgment, and the result was condemnation. But, in the other, countless men's sins are met with the free gift of grace, and the result is justification before God.

For if one man's offense meant that men should be slaves to death all their lives, it is a far greater thing that through another man, Jesus Christ, men by their acceptance of his more than sufficient grace and righteousness, should live all their lives like kings!

We see, then, that as one act of sin exposed the whole race of men to God's judgment and condemnation, so one act of perfect righteousness presents all men freely acquitted in the sight of God.

As death entered the world through a man, so has rising from the dead come to us through a man! As members of a sinful race all men die: as members of the Christ of God shall all men be raised to life, each in his proper order, with Christ the very first and after him all who belong to him when he comes.

It is written, moreover, that:

The first man Adam became a living soul. So the last Adam is a life-giving Spirit. But we should notice that the order is "natural" first and then "spiritual." The first man came out of the earth, a material creature. The second man came from Heaven and was the Lord himself. For the life of this world men are made like the material man; but for the life that is to come they are made like the one from Heaven.

We are citizens of Heaven; our outlook goes beyond this world to the hopeful expectation of the Savior who will come from Heaven, the Lord Jesus Christ. He will remake these wretched bodies of ours to resemble his own glorious body, by that power of his which makes him the master of everything that is.

Paul was no cold, logical academician, piling syllogism upon syllogism to arrive at an irrefutable, precise conclusion which ties together all loose ends and leaves no questions unanswered. He begins to state an argument calmly and lucidly, then expands his exposition into an elaborate analogy; his imagination soars, and he gets entangled in all kinds of inconsistencies which do violence to grammatical construction, let alone logical development. He starts again, often in mid-sentence, finds that language cannot bear the weight of the truth he is bursting to convey, stops and tries again. He is both teacher and poet, so it is little wonder that his critics found him wayward or thought him mentally confused. He was the prototype of a Bunyan rather than a Calvin. It was not that his mastery of language was inadequate; no vocabulary, however extensive, could express the wonder of his experience. He didn't always fail. His so-called Hymn to Love in I Corinthians 13 or his exposition of the Lordship of Christ, written to the Church at Philippi, reveals him as a magician with words combining the soul of a poet with the heart of a saint.

But underlying all his writings was a sense of urgency which would not allow him the luxury of long periods of reflection. Had he chosen the leisured protection of the cloister, the quietude of the library, he might have given birth to a systematic theology as comprehensive and massively consistent as that of Aquinas or Barth, but could he have been midwife to a universal Church?

An Anonymous Judaiser to Paul

Take note, blasphemer, of that word in Leviticus: "Whosoever names the name of the Lord shall be put to death."

Nonsense! The Truth Is Quite the Opposite!

Whosoever shall call upon the name of the Lord shall be saved.

That short exchange, probably merely one of a number of abusive notes Paul received from Jews who believed him to be a traitor to their faith, reminds us that Paul does not emerge from the mists of time, a man without any known past. Unlike an apologist like Justin Martyr or a theologian of the profundity of Origen, he does not speak of the Christian God as though a name had at last been found for the unknown absolute of pagan thought. Granted, at Mars Hill, he put a name to the unknown God whom the men of Athens had commemorated by a special altar: "The one whom you ignorantly worship, I now declare to you." But in general, Paul's Jewish background was an immense advantage to him. He had always believed in a living God, creator of Heaven and earth, and ruler of history. He inherited not only the stern tenets of the Law but also the prophetic insights concerning a God whose nature found expression in love and mercy. But for all his religious zeal, Paul had lived with a sense of failure. He confessed this to the Christians at Rome (a church he did not found) in the course of probably the only considered and polished theological pamphlet he ever wrote, as opposed to the hurried letters he dashed off to other churches:

The Jewish Law Trapped Me: Christ Released Me

It can scarcely be doubted that in reality the Law itself is holy, and the commandment is holy, fair, and good. Can it be that something that is intrinsically good could mean death to me? No, what happened was this. Sin, at the touch of the law, was forced to expose itself as sin, and that meant death for me. The contact of the law showed the sinful nature of sin.

My own behavior baffles me. For I find myself not doing what I really want to do but doing what I really loathe. Yet surely if I do things that I really don't want to do it cannot be said that "I" am doing them at all— it must be sin that has made its home in my nature. I often find I have the will to do good, but not the power. That is, I don't accomplish the good I set out to do, and the evil I don't really want to do I find I am always doing. When I come up against the law I want to do good, but in practice I do evil. My conscious mind wholeheartedly endorses the law, yet I observe an entirely different principle at work in my nature. This is in continual conflict with my conscious attitude, and makes me an unwilling prisoner to the law of sin and death. In my mind I am God's willing servant, but in my own nature I am bound fast, as I say, to the law of sin and death. It is an agonizing situation, and who on earth

107

can set me free from the clutches of my own sinful nature? I thank God there is a way out through Jesus Christ our Lord.

Dives to Paul   *Strictly Confidential*

My dear Paul,

The significance of my pseudonym will not have escaped you. I am a very rich man, and every time one of the apostles expounds that parable of the rich man and Lazarus I die a thousand deaths! And yet the extraordinary thing is that I found it possible either to keep the Law to the letter or else find a way round it without it interfering with my luxurious life—good food, the best of everything, and as a bonus a reputation for generosity towards the poor. I certainly didn't become a member of the Christian community in Rome out of any strong convictions. It was my aged mother who, though naturally comfortably off, was a lonely widow and was visited by Priscilla and Mary regularly (and not to solicit subscriptions but to give her companionship). She expressed the desire to share the worship and fellowship of the church, so naturally I took her along. The elders asked my advice about certain financial and land matters, so I just drifted in, as it were: a fat, jolly, rich Jew with, I confess, a tendency to sleep through the sermon.

But your very intimate, personal confession that you were always doing wrong when you desired to do right woke me up with a start! I, too, have the will to do good but don't seem to be able to summon the power to achieve it. Though I have a reputation for being easygoing and cheerful in my social life, my business competitors will tell you that I can be ruthless and drive hard bargains. So I live a double life, and deep down my conscience torments me. And the Law I was taught in the synagogue filled me with guilt, and I dreaded the Last Day when I would have to face God's wrath. That was probably my secret motive for leaving the synagogue and meeting Christians, who seemed to be able to believe in a God who is a Father, not just in the sense that he is the founder of our race but who surrounds his children with loving care.

I dearly want to believe that, and I would give up my fortune and beg in the streets if I thought it could be so. Your words have given me a little hope. Though our material circumstances have been so different, you and I seem to have traveled the same road. But whereas you have been able, through Christ, to subdue your lower nature, I am carnal through and through. What must I do to be saved?

I shall await anxiously your next exposition of the gospel to the Roman Church.

Dives

You Are Not Carnal if You Long for the Spirit

You are not carnal but spiritual if the Spirit of God finds a home within you. You cannot, indeed, be a Christian at all unless you have something of his Spirit in you. Now if Christ does live within you his presence means that your sinful nature is dead, but your spirit becomes alive because of the righteousness he brings with him. I said that our nature is "dead" in the presence of Christ, and so it is, because of its sin. Nevertheless once the Spirit of him who raised Jesus from the dead lives within you he will, by that same Spirit, bring to your whole being new strength and vitality. If you cut the nerve of your instinctive actions by obeying the Spirit, you are on the way to real living.

The Judge himself has declared us free from sin. Who

*is in a position to condemn? Only Christ, and Christ
died for us, Christ rose for us, Christ reigns in power for
us, Christ prays for us!*

Teaching of this sort was bound to put Paul at odds
with Jewish Christians, and especially the revered leaders
of the Church at Jerusalem. So far as his own Jewish
beliefs were concerned, he had gone beyond the point of
no return. The law had been repealed; its significance
being local and temporary. Gentiles could become Christians without fulfilling its obligations or performing its
rituals. His preaching offended not only Jews but also
some Jewish Christians on two main counts. To claim
that the law had been abrogated seemed to deny God's
promises to his chosen people. Even more repulsive to
Judaizers was his rejection of a legalistic God.

James, Son of Alpheus, to Paul

Paul!

Are you or are you not a Jew? Do you or do you
not belong to the chosen people? We are battling here
in Jerusalem to convert Jews to the way of Jesus and
encountering opposition from the Temple authorities.
So our job is hard enough without the constant rumors
which reach us of your teaching insulting the law and
belittling the Jewish past. Indeed, I wonder whether
we are serving the same God! I accept that some con-
cessions must be made to Gentiles—I was after all a
signatory to the Apostolic Decree! But you seem to be
starting your own religion. You are not a law unto
yourself, and you had better realize that you will have
a share of the responsibility if more of our leaders and
followers are martyred. We are not afraid to die, but
our deaths will have been in vain if we lead astray a

people who have had the one God for generations. We are plagued with enough sects. For God's sake, don't start another!

> Your fellow laborer,
> James

You Know My History—But Christ Has Wiped It Out

I was born a true Jew, I was circumcised on the eighth day, I was a member of the tribe of Benjamin, I was in fact a full-blooded Jew. As far as keeping the law is concerned I was a Pharisee, and you can judge my enthusiasm for the Jewish faith by my active persecution of the Church. As far as the law's righteousness is concerned, I don't think anyone could have found fault with me. Yet every advantage that I had gained I considered lost for Christ's sake. For his sake I did in actual fact suffer the loss of everything, but I considered it useless rubbish compared with being able to win Christ. For now my place is in him, and I am not dependent upon any of the self-achieved righteousness which comes from faith in Chirst.

James, Again, to Paul

Paul,

If only you would put some of that energy you once used in persecuting Christians in winning our fellow Jews, as well as Gentiles, to the Christian faith you would be held in much higher regard here. It seems that you feel it unnecessary to struggle as our forefathers did to meet God's strict requirements. Is Paul now so perfect that he needs no guidance from the law or the teaching of Jesus? Beware; remember that our Lord said he had come not to destroy the law but to fulfill it. Have you fulfilled it?

James

We Are Talking About Different Things!

How changed are my ambitions! Now I long to know Christ and the power shown by his Resurrection: now I long to share his sufferings, even to die as he died, so that I may perhaps attain, as he did, the resurrection from the dead. I do not consider myself to have "arrived," spiritually, nor do I consider myself already perfect. But I keep going on, grasping ever more firmly that purpose for which Christ grasped me. I do not consider myself to have fully grasped it even now. But I do concentrate on this: I leave the past behind and with hands outstretched to whatever lies ahead I go straight for the goal—my reward the honor of being called by God in Christ.

Such an exchange makes clear the differences between Paul and the leaders of the Jerusalem church. They shared in common the belief that "Christ died for our sins and rose again"—as Paul summarized it in one of his letters to the church of Corinth. But the other apostles do not seem to have fully realized the implications of this simple but breathtaking claim. Paul, however, had the foresight to see that the proclamation of Christ's death and resurrection transformed the whole range of religious experience, and, even more, involved a revolutionary new conception of the nature of God.

There remains one keystone of Paul's preaching which was, as he himself confessed, "a stumbling block to the

Jews" and "sheer nonsense" to the Greeks—the Cross of Christ.

Andronicus and Junia to Paul

Our dearest Paul,

Greetings from your very old friends and fellow missionaries! Like Aquila and Prisca, we still shock some of our Christian friends by traveling the face of the earth and preaching instead of staying in one place like most husbands and wives and raising a fine, big family to the glory of God!

We wish to consult you in the hope that you will be able to help us clarify our thinking and so add power to our preaching. We find a ready hearing for the teaching of Jesus, and his Resurrection has given many new hope. But many find his death upon the Cross either confusing or else frankly repulsive. Jews, of course, lose no opportunity of quoting Deuteronomy at us: "When a man is convicted of a capital offence and is put to death, you shall hang him on a gibbet; but his body shall not remain on the gibbet overnight; you shall bury it on the same day, for a hanged man is accursed in the sight of God." We know—we've been Christians long enough not only to understand Christ's death but also to glory in it. But we have hit a bad patch. We are being challenged by both Jews and Gentiles who, to be quite honest, are intellectually our superiors and also are more eloquent. Greek rhetoric at its best, like rabbinical scholarship, creates formidable opponents.

Did Christ suffer the actual curse of God? Did he bear the full weight of the divine anger for our sakes? If that is so, then it seems that it is penal justice and not grace which is the hallmark of God's rule over men. Hence, the law which you threw out of the window has come back through the door, for it looks as though Christ had to endure its curse in order to make God's grace available to men.

We know that it angers you when Christians claim that they are of the school of Paul or Peter or Apollos. But we must confess that we *are* of the school of Paul and firmly believe in your teaching of a gracious God who has rendered the law irrelevant through Christ. So however angry you may be with us for claiming you as our authority, please try to help us with this difficult matter.

Yours ever,
Andronicus and Junia

Start from This Point—Faith Precedes the Law

You can go right back to Abraham to see the principle of faith in God. He, we are told, "believed God and it was counted unto him for righteousness." Can you not see, then, that all those who "believe God" are the real "sons of Abraham"? The Scripture, foreseeing that God would justify the Gentiles "by faith," really proclaimed the gospel centuries ago in the words, "In thee shall all the nations be blessed." All men of faith share the blessing of Abraham.

Everyone, however, who is involved in trying to keep the law's demands falls under a curse, for it is written:

Cursed is every one that hangeth on a tree.

In all things *which are written in the book of the law,*

To do them.

It is made still plainer that no one is justified in God's sight by obeying the law, for:

The righteous shall live by faith.

And the law is not a matter of faith at all but of doing.

Now Christ has redeemed us from the curse of the law's condemnation, by himself becoming a curse for us when he was crucified. For the Scripture is plain: Cursed is every one that hangeth on a tree.

God's purpose is therefore plain: that the blessing promised to Abraham might reach the Gentiles through Jesus Christ, and the Spirit might become available to us all by faith.

But now we are seeing the righteousness of God declared quite apart from the law—it is a righteousness imparted to, and operating in, all who have faith in Jesus Christ. (For there is no distinction to be made anywhere: everyone has sinned, everyone has fallen short of the beauty of God's plan.) Under this divine "system" a man who has faith is now freely acquitted in the eyes of God by his generous dealing in the redemptive act of Jesus Christ. God has appointed him as the means of propitiation, a propitiation accomplished by the shedding of his blood, to be received and made effective in ourselves by faith. God has done this to demonstrate his righteousness both by the wiping out of the sins of the past, and by showing in the present time that he is a just God and that he justifies every man who has faith in Jesus Christ.

Paul belonged to a thoughtworld alien to our own. Terms such as "propitiation," "sacrifice," and "ransom" mean little to us, but they were the religious coinage of his time. In effect, Paul talking about Christ "becoming a curse" is using the law against itself. The "curse" which he mentions is obviously not the curse of God but the curse of the law, in the sense that accepting its terms of reference, anyone who died on a gibbet must be guilty of sin. But the law has failed because it condemned a righteous man. There is a rough analogy in the contemporary argument against capital punishment—only infallible men and an infallible system can apply it, for should they make a mistake it is irreparable, and so the law becomes the instrument of ultimate injustice. Equally, the law condemning Jesus proved its fallibility, and by implication demonstrated that God's sovereignty is not legalistic but expressed in vicarious sacrifice. So the death of Christ on the Cross has removed the curse of the law, for it is the supreme proof that God does not deal with the world in terms of strict recompense.

Andronicus and Junia to Paul Again

Dearest Paul,

Might we have a word or two of explanation of "righteousness of faith"? We are beginning to get the general drift of your thinking, but a little more light on this great idea would be welcome.

Yours, etc.

In a Word—God Takes the Initiative in Forgiving Sinners

If a man is in Christ he becomes a new person altogether—the past is finished and gone, everything has become fresh and new. All this is God's doing, for he has reconciled us to himself through Jesus Christ; and he has made us agents of the reconciliation. God was in Christ personally reconciling the world to himself—not counting their sins against them—and has commissioned us with the message of reconciliation.

Again, to understand Paul's meaning, we have to make the attempt to project ourselves back into the world in which he and the other missionaries of Christ of his generation moved. The key to man's attempt to get himself right with God was sacrifice, and oceans of blood flowed round primitive altars. Sacrifice was both a confession of man's estrangement from God and his attempt to set matters right. Paul, however, offers a revolutionry concept of "sacrifice"—the initiative comes from God's side. Here is a paradox which both Jews and pagans would find extraordinary if not shocking. The sacrifice is his own Son. So however mysterious the nature of God, what Paul makes clear is that there is no conflict within the Godhead between love and justice . . . men need not be the victims of divine punishment before love can have its way. All that men need to demonstrate is faith in Jesus, and they receive freely God's grace and forgiveness.

So Paul was, in a sense, proclaiming a new religion. He is trapped as we all are within the thoughtworld of our time, and a double translation is needed if we are to understand him fully—not only his Greek into English but also his ideas into concepts which make sense to us. But the master thought bursts out of his world into ours. Religion, founded upon Paul's understanding of God, is to be expressed not in the legalistic term of recompense but the loving attitude of reconciliation. And it is all God's doing, not ours. He is not dealing with the justice of the law courts, but with the grace of the Father who shows his love in the death of Christ.

And this is a truth to be experienced rather than explained.

5

Life in the Early Church

The Elders of the Church at Ephesus, to Paul

Dear Paul,

This letter comes to you with the official endorsement of the Church Council. It concerns our minister (and your friend) Timothy, about whom we have doubts as to his competence and gifts for the work to which both you and he feel he is called. Frankly, we have grave reservations. Ephesus, as you know, is one of the most strategic cities in the Empire, capital of the Proconsular Province of Asia and an important port and commercial center. We also boast, of course, one of the Seven Wonders of the World in the Temple of Diana. We hasten to add that though we have a legitimate pride in the architecture of this great edifice, we do not follow the official religion, though since the riots stirred up by Demetrius, the silversmith who felt Christians were causing widespread redundancy in the precious idol industry, we have taken great care to keep on good terms with Temple and civic officials.

It is precisely because our situation is so delicate that we feel that a more mature minister than Timothy is required here. He is an appallingly poor preacher—the older people who sit towards the back of the meeting house can't hear a single word he says, and what he does say lacks sound scholarship and that detailed knowledge of the Scriptures which our Jewish members in particular demand. Socially, too, he is so nervous and diffident that when he visits our members they find it a trial to entertain him. And naturally, the fact that he is of mixed blood makes him unacceptable in certain circles.

In short, we are writing to ask if you will give serious consideration to finding us another minister, whose gifts will reflect the importance of our church.

We are truly saddened to hear that you have been imprisoned again in Rome. If you are unable to visit us personally, possibly you might send Tychicus to discuss this delicate matter with us. Being from this part of the world, he is always received here with honor and listened to with respect.

We are,

Your fellow laborers at Ephesus

We Apostles Cannot Be All Things to All Men— but We Try!

Grace and peace be to you from God the Father and our Lord, Jesus Christ.

You all belong to one body, of which there is one Spirit, just as you all experienced one calling to one hope. There is one Lord, one baptism, one God, one Father of us all, who is the one over all, the one working through all and the one living in all.

119

Naturally there are different gifts and functions; individually grace is given to us in different ways out of the rich diversity of Christ's giving. His "gifts unto men" were varied. Some he made special messengers, some prophets, some preachers of the gospel; to some he gave the power to guide and teach his people. His gifts were made that Christians might be properly equipped for their service, that the whole body might be built up until the time comes when, in the unity of common faith and common knowledge of the Son of God, we arrive at real maturity—that measure of development which is meant by "the fullness of Christ."

Let there be no more resentment, no more anger or temper, no more violent self-assertiveness, no more slander, and no more malicious remarks. Be as ready to forgive others as God for Christ's sake has forgiven you.

I write that you may realize facts, as my dear children. After all, you may have ten thousand teachers in the Christian faith, but you cannot have many fathers! For in Jesus Christ I am your spiritual father through the gospel; that is why I implore you to follow the footsteps of me your father. I have sent Timothy to you to help you in this. For he himself is my much-loved and faithful son in the Lord, and he will remind you of those ways of living in Christ which I teach in every church to which I go.

Timothy was one of Paul's converts at Lystra. His mother, Eunice, was a Jewess; his father, a Gentile, whom Paul circumcised out of deference to the Jews who lived in that area. This was before Paul made his great decision to free Gentiles from the requirements of the Jewish Law— a decision which was to open up the whole world to the gospel. It is unlikely that Paul would take kindly to criticism of Timothy, who shared so many of the hazards, triumphs, and defeats of his missionary journeys. Hence, Paul to Timothy:

You Are a Minister! Prove It by Your Example

Don't let people look down on you because you are young: see that they look up to you because you are an example to them in your speech and behavior, in your love and faith and sincerity. Concentrate until my arrival on your reading and on your preaching and teaching. Never forget that you received the gift of proclaiming God's Word when the assembled elders laid their hands on you. Give your whole attention, all your energies, to these things, so that your progress is plain for all to see.

The ultimate aim of the Christian minister, after all, is to produce the love which springs from a pure heart, a good conscience, and a genuine faith.

Timothy, to Paul

Dearest Father in God,

I was frankly terrified when you put me in charge of the Christian community here in Ephesus. I started badly, and things have gotten steadily worse. I'll never make a preacher; never! No matter how carefully I prepare my sermons, the moment I see all those faces staring up at me, my legs turn to water and I stammer and stutter, losing my place in the manuscript and repeating myself over and over again. I'm afraid I'm not much credit to you. Ephesus, as you know well, is not short of cunning orators who knew every trick of the trade and draw the crowds. I'm no match for them in argument. They just run rings round me. And there are times when I am silent in the face of evil. It's not that I am afraid. I just can't think of anything to say until it is too late, so I'm scorned as either a fool or a coward.

The elders of the congregation are fully justified in their criticism of me, though in all charity, I do feel that some of them scorn me because I am of mixed race; and that cannot be right, for as you yourself have written, "In Christ there is neither Jew nor Gentile; all are one in him." There is the usual bickering and quarreling in the congregation that we experienced so often when I was traveling with you. But whereas you have the authority to rebuke and reprove, I just flounder, and I'm sure the followers of the goddess Diana, who are everywhere in this city, must think the Ambassador of King Jesus is a wooden donkey!

I am truly ashamed to send you such a dismal report of my progress while you are in prison. God works in a strange way. How much better it would be if I were in chains and you were free to preach the gospel! I might make a tolerable job of being a prisoner instead of being an utter failure as a minister. I fear constantly for your life, and I dearly wish our roles could be reversed. I'm sure I should find it easier to die for Christ than live for him.

Yours abysmally,
Timothy

Stick at It, Timothy

My son, be strong in the grace that Jesus Christ gives. Everything that you have heard me teach in public you should in turn entrust to reliable men, who will be able to pass it on to others.

I urge you, Timothy, as we live in the sight of God and of Christ Jesus (whose coming in power will judge the living and the dead), to preach the Word of God.

Never lose your sense of urgency, in season or out of season.

Stand fast in all that you are doing, meeting whatever suffering this may involve. Go on steadily preaching the gospel and carry out to the full the commission that God gave you.

I rely on this saying: If we died with him we shall also live with him: If we suffer with him we shall also reign with him. If we deny him he will also deny us: yet if we are faithless he always remains faithful. He cannot deny his own nature.

Set your heart not on riches, but on goodness, Christlikeness, faith, love, patience, and humility. Fight the worthwhile battle of the faith, keep your grip on that life eternal to which you have been called, and to which you boldly professed your loyalty before many witnesses.

Grace be with you

Elisabeth to Paul

Paul, Dear,

I feel I know you so well even though we have only met once. You may remember I was the young, well, early-middle aged lady who asked you that naughty question about evil thoughts on the occasion when that dreadful man, Alexander the coppersmith (common, horrid creature!) tried to break up your meeting. I thought you spoke so beautifully, and I've been a real fan of yours ever since. Why, O why don't we see more of you? We do so need your strong leadership in this wicked city with its sexual license and vice (of a kind I would blush to mention; what with Temple prostitutes and harlots who call themselves priestesses and unmentionable rites involving, so I'm told, animals —naturally I don't encourage talk about such things but one can't help hearing stories, can one?

It's really about Timothy, that shy, gentle creature, I'm writing to you. What a charming young man, and so devoted and loyal to you! He quotes you constantly in his lovely sermons. My heart aches for him. Everyone seems against him, but I've assured him that he is more than welcome in my household. Apart from anything else, it's so nice to be able to unburden oneself to a soul mate. That's what I feel we are—soul mates. My dear husband is a good man, but he is so wrapped up in his business that within minutes of arriving home from the office he's asleep in his chair and, frankly, just doesn't hear a word I say to him about my problems and innermost thoughts.

I regard myself as Timothy's right-hand man—silly me! right-hand woman, I should say. But so many of our so-called Christians here criticize and insult him that I don't know how the poor dear stands up to it all. He is so different from most of the other teachers who visit us from Jerusalem and terrify us with their lurid descriptions of Hell, warning us that we will suffer everlasting torment if we don't keep the letter of the Law. Poor Timothy! How he suffers. Please come and put these stern Judaizers in their place. Frankly, I fear for Timothy's sanity, let alone his health, if you don't help him. Please do come—and soon!

Timothy's sister in Christ, and your devoted follower,
Elisabeth

Beware of Neurotic Women and the Men Who Prey on Them

You must realize that in the last days the times will be full of danger. Men will become utterly self-centered,

*greedy for money, full of big words. They will be pas-
sionate and unprincipled, treacherous, self-willed and
conceited, loving all the time what gives them pleasure
instead of loving God. They will maintain a façade of
"religion," but their conduct will deny its validity.*

*From their number come those creatures who worm
their way into people's houses, and find easy prey in
silly women with an exaggerated sense of sin and morbid
cravings—who are always learning and yet never able
to grasp the truth.*

*Turn your back on the turbulent desires of youth and
give your positive attention to goodness, faith, love, and
peace in company with all those who approach God in
sincerity. Alexander the coppersmith did me a great deal
of harm—the Lord reward him for what he did—and I
should be very careful of him if I were you. He has been
an obstinate opponent of our teaching.*

Timothy to Paul

Dearest Father in God,

Thank you for your words of wise admonition. I
promise you, I am trying to be a faithful minister of
our Lord, but how can one preach the gospel when
he is constantly being persecuted by the very people
whom he ought to be able to count on for support?
And so many of the Jewish missionaries who visit our
community know so much more than I do about the
Law. They quote authorities I've never even heard of,
make claim to be descendants of the fathers of the
chosen people and will happily spend hours arguing
obscure issues which seem to me to have nothing to do
with the gospel. I'm afraid all the fight has gone out of
me, and I feel very low.

Hang On—and Stick to the Scriptures

*Persecution is inevitable for those who are deter-
mined to live really Christian lives, while wicked and
deceitful men will go from bad to worse, deluding others
and deluding themselves.*

*Yet you must go on steadily in those things that you
have learned and which you know are true. Remember
from what sort of people your knowledge has come, and
how from early childhood your mind has been familiar
with the holy Scriptures, which can open the mind to
the salvation which comes through believing in Christ
Jesus. All Scripture is inspired by God and is useful for
teaching the faith and correcting error, for resetting the
direction of a man's life and training him in good living.
The Scriptures are the comprehensive equipment of the
man of God, and fit him fully for all branches of his
work.*

According to Eusebius, who has been called the father of
church history, Timothy became the first Bishop of Ephesus
and was martyred for his public condemnation of the
licentious festivities associated with the goddess Diana.
Paul had long before received his reward, but Timothy's
change of role from a wandering missionary to the minister
of a settled Christian community prompts some comments
about the various styles of leadership in the early Church.
Paul was no bureaucrat. Though he is often caricatured as
a ticking bomb of compressed energy, fanatical in his zeal
and soulless in the ruthless discipline he imposed upon
himself and demanded of others, he seems, in fact, to have
shown little interest in formal organization. Every skill
and type of authority was a gift of God's grace rather than
the outworking of some primitive management theory. As
he told the Christians at Ephesus, God had richly endowed

his Church with a wide diversity of powers—each one a *charmisma*—a "grace-gift":

It Takes Many Gifts to Offer Christ's Fullness to the World

> *There is one Lord, one faith, one baptism, one God, one Father of us all, who is the one over all, the one working through all and the one living in all.*
>
> *Naturally there are different gifts and functions; individually grace is given to us in different ways out of the rich diversity of Christ's giving. Some he made special messengers, some prophets, some preachers of the gospel; to some he gave the power to guide and teach his people. His gifts were made that Christians might be properly equipped for their service, that the whole body might be built up until the time comes when, in the unity of common faith and common knowledge of the Son of God, we arrive at real maturity—that measure of development which is meant by "the fullness of Christ."*

Apostles, prophets, and teachers were the original officials of the Church. The office of teacher was taken over from the Jewish synagogue and involved expounding the Scriptures. The term "prophet," however, as it was used in the early Church, owed as much to Greek religion as to Hebrew tradition. Prophets led public worship and had a priestly role besides their better known function of reading the signs of the times and interpreting to men what God's Spirit was doing in the life of the world. The church at Antioch, which was not founded by Paul, had teachers and prophets and, according to the Acts, chose from its number two men to be "apostles" or missionaries. Heated argument raged about the term "apostle" because of Paul's insistence upon being included in their number even though he was not an official emissary from the Jerusalem church—which, for the purist, was the essential qualification to claim right to the title.

So two traditions existed side by side in the early Church concerning apostles. There was the Pauline model —naming as apostles those called by the Lord in person, as one of whom he regarded himself, and the older custom of designating every missionary as an apostle.

Judas of Corinth to Paul

Dear Paul,

I really must protest at your claim to be an Apostle, which is causing considerable controversy among some of our most influential Jewish Christians here. An "*a*postle"—yes; but an "*A*postle"—surely, only those leaders of the church at Jerusalem whom Jesus himself set apart and commissioned have any right to that great title? So far as I and many of our members here are concerned, we recognize you as an apostle in the same way that Andronicus, Junius, Stephanas, Fortunatus, and Achaicus are apostles. But if you insist on classing yourself with Peter, James, and the other nine at Jerusalem, then I'm afraid we cannot accord you such honor. Furthermore, how are we to tell true Apostles from false ones? Surely seniority must count for something! And the Eleven were witnessing for Christ while you were busy helping to put Stephen to death. Naturally, we've forgiven you for that, and we respect you as the foremost apostle to the Gentiles, but I will never accept your authority as an "Apostle," for if you, who never met Jesus, claim such a title, where will it all end? Frankly, I think I am as much an apostle as you are. I witness for Christ to both Jew and pagan alike, but I've no silly, inflated notions of my importance. I should have thought that your credentials ought to come from Antioch, where the mission to the Gentiles originated, rather than from Jerusalem.

After all, it was Barnabas whom the Jerusalem church sent to Antioch to lead the advance among the Gentiles. You were only his assistant. Now, to hear you talk, anyone would think you had dreamed up the whole idea of converting pagans to the way of Jesus! I happen to know that Barnabas is unhappy about many aspects of your teaching, and you ought to know that many of us share his unease. Jesus was a Jew. So is Barnabas. So are you. Have you become a traitor to your race, prepared to disobey the Law of Moses if it will make you popular among pagans?

Yours,

Judas (also an apostle!)

By Any Standard I Am an Apostle with a Capital "A"

Is there any doubt that I am a genuine special messenger, any doubt that I am a free man? Have I not seen Jesus our Lord with my own eyes? Are not you yourselves samples of my work for the Lord? Even if other people should refuse to recognize my divine commission, yet to you at any rate I shall always be a special messenger, for you are a living proof of God's call to me. This is my real ground of defense to those who cross-examine me.

I know a man in Christ who, fourteen years ago, had the experience of being caught up into the third heaven. I don't know whether it was an actual physical experience, only God knows that. All I know is that this man was caught up into paradise. This man heard words that cannot, and indeed must not, be translated into human speech. I am honestly proud of an experience like that, but I have made up my mind not to boast of anything personal, except of what may be called my weaknesses. I am not really in the least inferior, nobody as I am, to these extraspecial special messengers. You have had an exhaustive demonstration of the power God gives to a genuine messenger in the miracles, signs and works of spiritual power that you saw with your own eyes.

I am the least of the special messengers, and indeed I do not deserve that title at all, because I persecuted the Church of God. But what I am now I am by the grace of God. The grace he gave me has not proved a barren gift. I have worked harder than any of the others —and yet it was not I but this same grace of God within me.

Judas Again, to Paul

What's all this business of having "seen" Jesus? How could that be? You could know *of* him, but how could you have known him? We lesser apostles know of him and lose no opportunity of telling others about him. But you seem to have founded some religion made up of a hodgepodge of ideas taken from all kinds of sources. I'm sure the true Apostles would repudiate much of your teaching, and if your teaching varies from theirs, how can you class yourself with them?

Judas

To Know of Jesus Won't Do: You Must Be "in" Him

I am a minister of the Church by divine commission, a commission granted to me for your benefit and for a special purpose: that I might fully declare God's Word —that sacred mystery which up till now has been hidden in every age and every generation, but which is now as clear as daylight to those who love God. They are those to whom God has planned to give a vision of the full wonder and splendor of his secret plan for the sons of men. And the secret is this: Christ in you! Yes, Christ in you bringing with him the hope of all the glorious things to come.

How I long for you to grow more certain in your knowledge and more sure in your grasp of God himself! May your spiritual experience become richer as you see more and more fully God's great secret, Christ himself! For it is in him, and in him alone, that men will find all the treasures of wisdom and knowledge.

Paul had become an apostle without having been a disciple in the strictest historical sense of sitting at the feet of Jesus of Nazareth. The Christ with whom he felt himself united was the Risen Lord, and, in particular, the Lord of the Church. The Church was the agent though not the source of his conversion. Unfashionable the term may seem, but Paul was a churchman. His apostolate was not exercised in isolation but within and through the Church. So questions concerning the degrees and types of authority by which the Church was governed were matters to which he had to give attention. Apostles, prophets, and teachers served Christendom as a whole; their authority was accepted throughout all the churches, but every movement as it expands necessarily becomes an organization in a particular place and demands some kind of permanent overseer—a local minister. Paul uses a number of titles for such ministers: helpers, leaders, presidents, servants, and "those who show mercy." But in the opening greeting to the Christians at Philippi, he uses two terms which have survived the test of time, "bishops" and "deacons." In Paul's time, the organization was the minimum required for the effective preaching of the gospel and the care of Christians. The Church's unity seemed for Paul not to be vested in any uniformity of organization but to be based upon the common possession of the Spirit demonstrated in the love of each for all.

Theodosius to Paul

Dear Paul,

This stripling, Timothy, whom you misguidedly put in charge of the church at Ephesus, has passed me over in appointing our bishops. I have no worldly ambition, but I do have considerable business experience, and I was considered worthy to be an elder in the synagogue before I became a Christian. I have served the church here devotedly for a long time, and my opinions are widely respected. It is true that I have opposed many of Timothy's policies, but I can assure you I am not alone in this! I am a pillar of this church, and I will not be ordered about by someone half my age; and a half-caste at that!

Please rectify this disastrous action at once, not to pander to my personal pride—my good works speak for themselves—but to save the Church from ruin.

Your elder brother in Christ,
Theodosius

It's Character Not Seniority That Counts

For the office of a bishop a man must be of blameless reputation, he must be married to one wife only, and be a man of self-control and discretion. He must be a man of disciplined life; he must be hospitable and have the gift of teaching. He must be neither intemperate nor violent, but gentle. He must not be a controversialist nor must he be fond of money-grabbing. He must have proper authority in his own household and be able to control and command the respect of his children. (For if a man cannot rule in his own house how can he look after the Church of God?) He must not be a beginner in the faith, for fear of his becoming conceited and sharing Satan's downfall. He should, in addition to the above qualifications, have a good reputation with the outside world, in case his good name is attacked and he is caught by the devil that way. It makes no difference what your earthly status is—God pays no regard to the externals of men. Please God it will not be long before I come to you in person and take the measure of self-important people, not by what they say, but by what power is in them.

Theodosius Again, to Paul

Dear Paul,

Since I last wrote to you, Timothy has added insult to injury by offering to appoint me a deacon! A deacon, if you please! A common waiter at tables and a nursemaid to the sick. If that is all he thinks I am worth, I shall resign all my various offices, particularly the treasurership, and then see how they get on without me. No answer is required: I need no lecture on how to behave.

Theodosius

Lucius to Paul

My dear Paul,

I felt I must write and give you the good news. I have been appointed a deacon! It is an overwhelming honor, especially since I've been a Christian for so short a time. I swear before God that I will do everything in my power to justify the confidence the Church has placed in me. To serve my fellow Christians in no matter how menial a way is my great desire. I'm not very bright, and I have no skill as a teacher, but I am a practical sort of man, and I'll tend the sick and visit those who cannot attend worship. To share in the administration of the Lord's Supper and take the bread and wine to the homes of the people is a privilege I do not deserve, but I will try to assist the bishops in every possible way. I can't do great things like Timothy, but I can knock a nail in a wall or dig a garden to the glory of God.

Your servant,
Lucius

We Can't All Lead, But We Can All Serve

In any big household there are naturally not only gold and silver vessels but wooden and earthenware ones as well. Some are used for the highest purposes and some for the lowest. If a man keeps himself clean from the contaminations of evil he will be a vessel used for honorable purposes, clean and serviceable for the use of the master of the household, all ready, in fact, for any good purpose. Take the greatest care of the good things which were entrusted to you by the Holy Spirit who lives within you.

What form did the worship of the early Church take? What did Christians say and sing and do? The power and freedom of the Spirit swept like a tidal wave through the solemn assemblies, upsetting formal liturgies. There were those present who had caught a glimpse of visions no human eye could see and listened to what no human ear had ever heard; they spoke what was higher than human reason; worked miracles, healed the sick, cast out demons, and orchestrated a chorus of joy. They presided, in fact, at a Festival of the Spirit. What order there was came from a fusion of the rites of the synagogue and the commemoration of the Upper Room. Men were bareheaded and women veiled, and they were separated as in Jewish worship:

A Group in Macedonia to Paul

Dear Paul,

One of our number heard you preaching the gospel of Jesus when you passed along our coast on your way to Greece. He was fired with zeal to establish a Christian community here; and now there are seven of us. We meet in Demos's house on the Lord's Day and the Spirit is with us. But we are anxious that our worship and practice should be in line with that of the Church in every other place, so that we do not stray into error or form some strange sect of which you would not approve. So here we are. What ought we to do when we meet to celebrate the Lord's death until he returns?

Respectfully,

Demos and six others

Do What the Spirit Commands, but Decently and in Order

Never damp the fire of the Spirit, and never despise what is spoken in the name of the Lord. Whenever you meet let everyone be ready to contribute a psalm, a piece of teaching, a spiritual truth, or a "tongue" with an interpreter. Supplications, prayers, intercessions, and thanksgivings should be made on behalf of all men: for kings and rulers in positions of responsibility, so that our common life may be lived in peace and quiet, with a proper sense of God and of our responsibility to him for what we do with our lives. I passed on to you the message I had myself received—that Christ died for our sins, as the Scriptures said he would; that he was buried and rose again on the third day, again as the Scriptures foretold. The rising of Christ from the dead is the very heart of our message. As far as the Fund for Christians in Need is concerned, I should like to follow the same rule that I gave to the Galatian church. Put so much aside to be sent to Jerusalem.

Thus far, Christian worship could be described as a modified form of the rites of the synagogue—excepting, of course, the confession of faith in the Risen Lord. But then, as they say, the fun begins—with this question of speaking in tongues. It is ironic that the Corinthian church, the conduct of some of whose members was a public scandal, raised the issue most acutely:

Titus to Paul

My dear Paul,

According to your instructions I am at Corinth, which has the strangest church I have ever had the misfortune to visit. I truly think these Corinthians are mad! I could write a book about their excesses and peculiarities, but there is a specific issue which I feel needs your urgent attention—this matter of "speaking in tongues" —the ecstatic utterance of gibberish—words that have no meaning in any language known to man. I know this practice has been since Pentecost a sign of Spirit-possession, but I truly believe the whole thing has got out of hand here and needs the strongest possible guidance from you personally. I would plead that you give this matter your most urgent attention and lay down some rules before the whole church here becomes a howling Babel. All we need is the tower: we've got the incoherent babbling which brought it crashing!

Your son,
Titus

Let's Put "Speaking in Tongues" into Perspective

The highest gift you can wish for is to be able to speak the messages of God. The man who speaks in a "tongue" addresses not men (for no one understands a word he says) but God; and only in his spirit is he speaking spiritual secrets. But he who preaches the word of God is using his speech for the building up of the faith of one man, the encouragement of another or the consolation of another. The speaker in a "tongue" builds up his own soul, but the preacher builds up the Church of God.

I should indeed like you all to speak with "tongues," but I would much rather that you all preached the word of God. For the preacher of the word does a greater work than the speaker with "tongues," unless of course the latter interprets his words for the benefit of the Church.

In the Law it is written:

By men of strange tongues and by the lips of strangers will I speak unto this people: and not even thus will they hear me, saith the Lord.

That means that tongues are a sign of God's power, not for those who are unbelievers but to those who already believe. Preaching the word of God, on the other hand, is a sign of God's power to those who do not believe rather than to believers. So that, if at a full church meeting you are all speaking with tongues and men come in who are both uninstructed and without faith, will they not say that you are insane? But if you are preaching God's word and such a man should come in to your meeting, he is convicted and challenged by your united speaking of the truth. His secrets are exposed, and he will fall on his knees acknowledging God and saying that God is truly among you!

Babilos of Corinth to Paul

Dear Paul,

It is universally accepted here at Corinth that I have been given a greater measure of power to speak with tongues than anyone else in the church. God be praised for that! When the Spirit takes hold of me I can utter the very language of heaven; words that no ordinary man can understand. Have you forgotten Pentecost? You seem to belittle what has been, from the beginnings of the Church, the supreme expression of possession by the Holy Spirit. Your emissary, Titus, possibly because he lacks this great gift, does everything possible to undermine my witness. But I shall continue to speak words that no mortal man can understand when I am so inspired. I had always understood that you had the gift of "prophecy," but, frankly, I am beginning to wonder.

Babilos

I Can Beat You at Your Own Game, but What Is the Point?

I thank God that I have a greater gift of "tongues" than any of you, yet when I am in church I would rather speak five words with my mind (which might teach something to other people) than ten thousand words in a "tongue" which nobody understands.

Because of the revival of the charismatic movement in the modern Church, it is important to give some attention to the way Paul regarded it in the early Church and the rules he laid down, the warning note he sounded, and the place he saw for ecstatic utterance. He certainly did not forbid these highly emotional and unintelligible speeches, but he made it very clear that ecstasy is, in itself, no proof of truth. As he told the Christians at Corinth:

A Warning, Some Advice, and a Declaration

Suppose I came to you, my brothers, speaking with "tongues," what good could I do you unless I could give you some revelation of truth, some knowledge in spiritual things, some message from God, or some teaching about the Christian life?

Unless the bugle note is clear who will be called to arms? So, in your case, unless you make intelligible sounds with your "tongue" how can anyone know what you are talking about? If one of your number speaks with a "tongue," he should pray that he may be able to interpret what he says.

If I pray in a "tongue" my spirit is praying, but my mind is inactive. I am therefore determined to pray with my spirit and my mind, and if I sing I will sing with both spirit and mind. Otherwise, if you are blessing God with your spirit, how can those who are ungifted say amen to your thanksgiving, since they do not know what you are talking about? If the question of speaking with a "tongue" arises, confine the speaking to two or three at the most and have someone to interpret what is said. If you have no interpreter then let the speaker with a "tongue" keep silent in the church and speak only to himself and God.

Never damp the fire of the Spirit.

Babilos, yet Again

Paul,

You tell us not to damp the fire of the Spirit, but all the rules and regulations you lay down about speaking in tongues are likely to do just that. It's the old Pharisee in you, obsessed with the dead law rather than the living Spirit. We have joy and freedom when we abandon ourselves to the Spirit. You would have us go back to the old, boring rituals of the synagogue. Well, we have started a spiritual revolution here, and there is nothing you can do to stop it!

Babilos

The Spirit Has Many Gifts, and Tongues Is Not the Greatest

*Men have different gifts, but it is the same Spirit
who gives them. There are different ways of serving
God, but it is the Lord who is served. God works
through different men in different ways, but it is the
same God who achieves his purposes through them all.*

*Each man is given his gift by the Spirit—that he may
make the most of it.*

*One man's gift by the Spirit is to speak with wisdom,
another's to speak with knowledge. The same Spirit
gives to another man faith, to another the ability to
heal, to another the power to do great deeds. The same
Spirit gives to another man the gift of preaching the
word of God, to another the ability to discriminate in
spiritual matters, to another speech in different tongues,
and to yet another the power to interpret the tongues.*

*You should set your hearts on the highest spiritual
gifts, but I will show you what is the highest way of
all. Follow, then, the way of love, while you set your
heart on the gifts of the Spirit. The highest gift you
can wish for is to be able to speak the messages of God.*

*The Spirit produces in human life fruits such as
these: love, joy, peace, patience, kindness, generosity,
fidelity, adaptability, and self-control.*

So Paul, without denying the validity of ecstatic speech,
was, by his firm insistence that it was only one expression
of the Spirit, and a minor one at that, able to prevent
Christianity from the ever-present peril of becoming yet
another orgiastic cult in the pagan world. Life in the
Spirit indeed created a revolution, but the liberty it offered
was not that of the Stoics, as defined by Cicero: "What
is Freedom? The power of living as you will." Ecstatic
speech, genuinely inspired by the Spirit did not reveal

esoteric secrets; make fresh revelations about the nature of God—its purpose was to confirm the revelation already given in Christ.

What of the other two key elements in Christian worship, baptism and the Lord's Supper? Take baptism. Jesus was himself baptized by John, and his first recruits were followers of the Baptist. Then we hear no more of the practice except for the missionary commission of Jesus, recorded in all four Gospels and expressed in Mark as "Go forth into every part of the world and proclaim the good news to the whole creation. Those who believe it and receive it will find salvation; those who do not believe it will be condemned" (NEB). Yet the young Christian Church from its beginnings had a baptismal usage which antedates the conversion of Paul. So he did not revive the practice, but as a missionary continued it.

Baptism has a decisive role in a missionary church. It is the setting within which the convert stands up to be counted. Before, he may have been a sympathetic onlooker, undecided, wistful, or confused, still part of that half-world of gods and demons which rule his pagan environment. Once baptized, he has the mark of Christ on him. It is not going too far to claim that in every convert's history there is a grave and a resurrection—as Paul reminds the church at Rome:

Remember Your Baptism: It Is an End and a Beginning

We, who have died to sin—how could we live in sin a moment longer? Have you forgotten that all of us who were baptized into Jesus Christ were, by that very action, sharing in his death? We were dead and buried with him in baptism, so that just as he was raised from the dead by that splendid revelation of the Father's power so we too might rise to life on a new plane alto-

gether. If we have, as it were, shared his death, let us rise and live our new lives with him!

Elephas to Paul

Dear Paul,

I am writing to ask a favor of you. My brother, after a long spiritual struggle, has decided to join the church here. Since he is widely known in the Cenchreae area (he is in fact the Deputy Chief Harbor Pilot) I am most anxious that he should become a real Christian and not get involved with these cliques who by their behavior and belief seem to me to be utterly heretical about many aspects of the faith. I was wondering therefore whether you would be prepared to baptize him yourself on your next visit so that he will get off to a good start. Don't be falsely modest. This is *your* church (under Christ of course), and though I myself was baptized by others—since you were in prison at the time— I count myself as one of your disciples, cherish your teaching, and quote you constantly in debate against the factions which, in my view, Cephas, Apollos, and others have deliberately encouraged.

Could you give me some idea when you might be passing this way again? I will then make the necessary arrangements.

Yours always,
Elephas

Don't Drag My Name into Your Petty Disputes!

What are you saying? Is there more than one Christ? Was it Paul who died on the Cross for you? Were you baptized in the name of Paul? It makes me thankful that I didn't actually baptize any of you (except Crispus and Gaius), or perhaps someone would be saying I did it in my own name. (Oh yes, I did baptize Stephanas' family, but I can't remember anyone else.) For Christ did not send me to see how many I could baptize, but to proclaim the gospel.

Isaac to Paul

I am an uncircumcised Jew, now a committed Christian. There are two parties in this church: one claims that I must be circumcised, as were the elders of the Jerusalem church, the other quotes you as saying that the law and circumcision have ceased to matter. What is the truth? I am prepared to undergo circumcision if I must, but I value the freedom I have in Christ from the old religion.

Your servant,
Isaac

Baptism Is to the Christian What Circumcision Was to the Jew

In Christ you were circumcised, not by any physical act, but by being set free from the sins of the flesh by virtue of Christ's circumcision. This circumcision sets you free not just from some sins but from the whole carnal body. This circumcision you have because you were buried with Christ to your old self beneath the waters of baptism, and were raised with him from these same waters to a new and regenerate life, through your faith in the powerful working of God who raised him from the dead.

Isaac Again, to Paul

Father—I must confess. I have faith in Christ but I am ashamed to say that not only am I uncircumcised but I have not been baptized either. Have I been living a lie? I am, you see, an orphan, a child of the streets, so I was not circumcised, and because I do not know my parents I could not declare myself in the Christian community. I listened and prayed from afar. But I truly believe.

Isaac

Baptism Does Not Create Faith: It Is Symbol of It

Note this carefully. We began by saying that Abraham's faith was counted unto him for righteousness. When this happened, was he a circumcised man? He was not, he was still uncircumcised. It was afterwards *that the sign of circumcision was given to him, as a seal upon that righteousness which God was accounting to him* as yet an uncircumcised man! *God's purpose here is twofold. First, that Abraham might be the spiritual father of all who since that time, despite their uncircumcision, show the faith that is counted as righteousness. Then, secondly, that he might be the circumcised father of all those who are not only circumcised, but are living by the same sort of faith which he himself had before he was circumcised.*

For Paul, then, baptism was the marking of a man in the name of the crucified Jesus, a truth the early Church symbolized by making the sign of the Cross over the person to be baptized. But God retains his sovereign initiative —even over his Church and its sacrament. Salvation is not inextricably bound up with baptism. There can be baptism without the Spirit, and the Spirit can claim a person who is unbaptized because it "blows where it chooses." In the last resort, only the Lord knows those who belong to him. So baptism is the norm, but it is not the invariable qualification for belonging to the community of faith.

Rabbi Michel to Paul

Sir,

Are you aware that your followers in this city are practicing a parody of the Passover which is both a dishonoring of the Sacred Name and equally an offense to my congregation? There is no lamb, no unleavened bread, nor the four cups prescribed in the ritual, but a single cup. Furthermore, this strange rite is not confined to the time of the Passover but seems to take place as frequently as our *kiddush* which, as you ought to know, is held on the eve of the Sabbath and feast days.

If your followers are celebrating some form of *kiddush,* then it is my duty to inform you that there are a number of irregularities taking place which the President of the Sanhedrin at Jerusalem demands should stop; and that your practice should be brought into line with that of the congregations under their jurisdiction.

Shalom,
Michel

Paul answered the Rabbi's charges in his instructions to the church at Corinth:

Jesus Is the Lamb and His Followers the Unleavened Bread

Your pride in your church is lamentably out of place. Don't you know how a little yeast can permeate the

*whole lump? Clear out every bit of the old yeast that
you may be new unleavened bread! We Christians have
had a Passover Lamb sacrificed for us—none other than
Christ himself! So let us "keep the feast" with no trace
of the yeast of the old life, nor the yeast of vice and
wickedness, but with the unleavened bread of unadulterated truth!*

So instead of a Passover lamb, Jesus was the perpetual
sacrifice: Good Friday was therefore the Passover festival
of all history. And Paul regarded true followers of Jesus
as the "unleavened bread" of unadulterated ethical purity.
But there were Gentiles, accustomed to pagan feasts, who,
in the jargon of the racecourse, wanted to back the horse
both ways, by attending celebrations of the Lord's Supper
and also retaining their old associations by attending the
rituals of the mystery religions. Paul put the choice to
them starkly:

You Must Drink to God or the Devil, but Not Both

*The lesson we must learn, my brothers, is at all costs
to avoid worshiping a false God. I am speaking to you
as intelligent men: think over what I am saying.*

*The cup of blessing which we bless, is it not a very
sharing in the blood of Christ? When we break the
bread do we not actually share in the body of Christ?
The very fact that we all share one bread makes us all
one body.*

*Now am I implying that a false god really exists, or
that sacrifices made to any god have some value? Not
at all: I say emphatically that Gentile sacrifices are made
to evil spiritual powers and not to God at all. I don't
want you to have any fellowship with such powers. You
cannot drink both the cup of the Lord and the cup of
devils. You cannot be a guest at the Lord's table and*

at the table of devils. *Are we trying to arouse the wrath of God? Have we forgotten how completely we are in his hands?*

Hannah to Paul

Dear Paul,

I have just returned from Jerusalem, where my husband was privileged to attend a gathering for the Lord's Supper. The President in his address made it clear that they were meeting to have table fellowship with the Risen Lord. It was a simple memorial meal. I must confess I returned not a little perturbed that you seem to regard the Lord's Supper as much more than a commemoration. When you write of "sharing the body and blood of Christ" are you not straying from the intention of the apostles? Are you not implying that in our Lord's Supper we are "eating our god"—to my mind, a barbaric idea which even Marcus Tullius Cicero was condemning long before Jesus was even born? He wrote, "When we call grain Ceres or wine Liber, we merely use a common style of speech, but do you think anyone is so insane as to suppose what he eats is God?"

If you do not follow the practice of the apostles, where did the teaching you have given to us come from? Surely not from the mystery religions? I am very worried and need reassurance that we are not turning Jesus into a pagan deity.

Your sister in Christ,
Hannah

My Teaching Comes from Revelation Not Imitation

The teaching I give you was given to me personally by God himself, and it was this: the Lord Jesus, in the same night in which he was betrayed, took bread, and when he had given thanks he broke it and said, "Take, eat, this is my body which is being broken for you. Do this in remembrance of me." Similarly, when supper was ended, he took the cup saying, "This cup is the new agreement in my blood: do this, whenever you drink it, in remembrance of me."

This can only mean that whenever you eat this bread or drink of this cup, you are proclaiming that the Lord has died for you, and you will do that until he comes again. So that, whoever eats the bread or drinks the wine without due thought is making himself like one of those who allowed the Lord to be put to death without discerning who he was.

Marcellus Gallius to Paul

Paul, old man,

I'm regarded in these parts as a bit of a gay blade; must confess I'm partial to the ladies and a bottle or two of good wine. But I think I can claim to be basically a decent sort of fellow. It's just my military background that's gotten me into the habit of enjoying the better things of life. Can't pretend to be very partial to the old hymn singing and that sort of thing. But I never miss the Lord's Supper—never! I feel that whatever I've done that's, well, you know, not up to the mark—I can get it off my chest and start off again with a clean slate. You must admit that the Christian life is a bit of a drag if you have to stick to the rules, but rather than keep a score of all my little indulgences, I confess the lot at the Lord's Supper and go happily on my way. There are one or two of the elders who seem to make it a full-time occupation to lecture me and tell me I ought to mend my ways—though I'm not sure whether it's their concern for my soul or envy at my exploits that keeps them nagging at me.

But it is all right, isn't it, so long as I attend the Lord's Supper? All these rules and restrictions make for a pretty dull life, and Jesus *did* want us to be happy. So I thought I'd just drop a line to the old brigadier, as it were, to confirm that I'm on the right track.

Your respectfully,
Marcellus Gallius

You Are Playing a Deadly Dangerous Game

No, a man should thoroughly examine himself, and only then should he eat the bread or drink of the cup. He that eats and drinks carelessly is eating and drinking a judgment on himself, for he is blind to the presence of the Lord's body. It is this careless participation which is the reason for the many feeble and sickly Christians in your church, and the explanation of the fact that many of you are spiritually asleep.

If we were closely to examine ourselves beforehand, we should avoid the judgment of God. But when God does judge us, he disciplines us as his own sons, that we may not be involved in the general condemnation of the world.

In rebuking the church at Corinth, Paul conveyed a profound understanding of the meaning of the Lord's Supper: it was more than a ritual memorial of the death of Jesus. It was a sacrificial meal, since those who took part in it entered into a mystical fellowship with one another and with the Risen Lord, whose real presence at the table transformed them into the spiritual body which was at one and the same time that of the Church and of Christ himself. For Paul, as for John Wesley, the Lord's Supper was an evangelical office—by our willingness or otherwise to enter into the death of Christ we are either saved or judged.

6

Pastoral Paul

Love—Christ's Abiding Gift to Me

If I were to speak with the combined eloquence of men and angels I should stir men like a fanfare of trumpets or the crashing cymbals, but unless I had love, I should do nothing more. If I had the gift of foretelling the future and had in my mind not only all human knowledge but the secrets of God, and if, in addition, I had that absolute faith which can move mountains, but had no love, I tell you I should amount to nothing at all. If I were to sell all my possessions to feed the hungry and, for my convictions, allowed my body to be burned, and yet had no love, I should achieve precisely nothing.

This love of which I speak is slow to lose patience—it looks for a way of being constructive. It is not possessive: it is neither anxious to impress nor does it cherish inflated ideas of its own importance.

Love has good manners and does not pursue selfish advantage. It is not touchy. It does not compile statistics of evil or gloat over the wickedness of other people. On the contrary, it is glad with all good men when truth prevails.

Love knows no limit to its endurance, no end to its trust, no fading of its hope; it can outlast anything. It is, in fact, the one thing that still stands when all else has fallen.

In this life we have three lasting qualities—faith, hope, and love. But the greatest of them is love.

An Anonymous Christian to Paul

My dear Paul,

You don't know me. There is no reason why you should. I rarely go to church, though I do try to be there when I hear that they are reading out one of your letters. You always write such good sense. I was in church the other week when you gave us your exposition of the nature of true love—the love of Christ. Frankly, it hit me dead-center. I feel I must write to you out of gratitude and sorrow—gratitude, because you brought me face to face with a truth I have been trying to avoid, and sorrow, because I now realize what an awful mess I've made, not only of my own life, but of someone else's as well.

I really thought I loved someone very deeply before you exposed my feelings for what they really were— sheer egotism and selfishness. I have been unwilling, or, more likely, afraid to allow the one I love to be herself for fear she would desert me. Far from being good-mannered and forbearing, our relationship has been one never-ending brawl with displays of temper, jealousy, and moodiness on my part. I thought that my bouts of fury were proof of the intensity of my love, but in fact I now see that they were devices to bind her to me. I was prepared to make any sacrifice for her except the one which really mattered, willingness to trust myself to her without any guarantees or safeguards. I was always wanting reactions to prove that my love was returned. I constantly put her to the test. I just didn't see that what I was demanding could only be given to me freely or not at all. In the name of my so-called love I have committed all kinds of sins: pride, envy, ill-temper, suspicion, and lust. Eventually, she could take no more and has gone—where, I have no idea.

My life is in ruins, and what is worse, I know I have ruined someone else's life. My past haunts me and the future seems just empty. Oh, I could find another woman, but it would be the same thing all over again. Is this what I am condemned to—a life of "more of the same"? Having realized how loveless a person I am, I have no right to expect anyone, let alone God, to love me.

Please don't bother to reply to this letter; I know what an important and busy man you are. But dare I ask that when you next write to the church here, you might say something, anything, to assure someone as pathetically lost as myself that there might be a second chance? If not I shall quite understand.

Yours,
Someone Who Had Better Remain Nameless

No One Is Denied a New Beginning in Christ

For if a man is in Christ he becomes a new person al-together—the past is finished and gone, everything has become fresh and new. Because God was in Christ personally reconciling the world to himself—not count-ing their sins against them!

Thank God, then, for his indescribable generosity to you.

The grace that comes through our Lord Jesus Christ, the love that is of God the Father, and the fellowship that is ours in the Holy Spirit be with you all!

The Treasurer of the Church at Jerusalem to Paul

Dear Paul,

We are greatly concerned at the considerable falling off of funds transmitted to the Mother Church from several Christian communities under your charge. It is not for me to make unsubstantiated accusations against a Christian brother, but we can only conclude that you have been using the gifts of the altar as fees for your teaching ministry. You will appreciate that if this practice became widespread among our missionaries we should be unable to set aside funds for the building of a splendid church we have it in mind to name after Peter.

I would be grateful for some statement of account as soon as possible, and also the reassurance that you still maintain the tradition of the worker-rabbi (tentmaking, I think) and have not become a paid sophist like the Greek philosophers.

Yours expectantly,

Judas Ben Joseph

The Treasurer of the Church at Corinth to Paul

Dear Paul,

I am writing at the instigation of a group of elders who are very concerned at your refusal to accept from our people any financial help to support your work among us. As you know it is the practice of the Greek teachers to charge for their services, and there's no doubt, as I always say in my business, people only value what they pay for. So there is a tendency among some of our Greek Christians to feel that your teaching can't be of much value if you are giving it away free. We also have others who feel offended at the way in which you have refused their well-meant gifts; "Paul," they say, "isn't really interested in our welfare!" That is not the general view, of course, but you will appreciate that in a largely pagan city, non-Jews tend to look down upon a rabbi who works with his hands, and this reflects upon us all.

I have opened a special fund so that those who wish to do so can contribute something towards the upkeep of Barnabas and yourself. Please make use of it.

Sincerely,

David

Treasurer, Corinth Church Council

I Just Can't Win, Can I?

Perhaps I made a mistake in cheapening myself (though I did it to help you) by preaching the gospel without a fee? As a matter of fact I was only able to do this by "robbing" other churches, for it was what they paid me that made it possible to minister to you free of charge. Even when I was with you and very hard up, I did not bother any of you. It was the brothers who came from Macedonia who brought me all that I needed. Yes, I kept myself from being a burden to you then, and so I intend to do in the future.

Does this mean that I do not love you? God knows it doesn't. If I do this work because I choose to do so then I am entitled to a reward. But if it is no choice of mine, but a sacred responsibility put upon me, what can I expect in the way of reward? This, that when I preach the gospel, I can make it absolutely free of charge, and need not claim what is my rightful due as a preacher. For though I am no man's slave, yet I have made myself everyone's slave, that I might win more men to Christ.

Paul was obviously angered by the refusal of the Judaizers from the Jerusalem church to recognize his status as an apostle, and particularly by their objection that he had, occasionally, when down on his luck, accepted some financial help—though rarely. He insisted that he had as much right as any other apostle to wages, even though he chose not to exercise that right:

Even a Missionary Must Eat!

Aren't we allowed to eat and drink? May we not travel with a Christian sister like the other special messengers, like other Christian brothers, and like Cephas? Are Barnabas and I the only ones not allowed to leave their ordinary work to give time to the ministry? Our struggles and hard work, my brothers, must be still fresh in your minds. Day and night we worked so that our preaching of the gospel to you might not cost you a penny.

Just think for a moment. Does any soldier ever go to war at his own expense? Does any man plant a vineyard and have no share in its fruits? Does the shepherd who tends the flock never taste the milk? This is, I know an argument from everyday life, but it is a principle endorsed by the law. For is it not written in the Law of Moses:

Thou shalt not muzzle the ox when he treadeth out the corn?
Now does this imply merely God's care for oxen, or

does it include his care for us too? Surely we are included! You might even say that the words were written for us.

Are you ignorant of the fact that those who minister sacred things take part of the sacred food of the Temple for their own use, and those who attend the altar have their share of what is placed on the altar? On the same principle the Lord has ordered those who proclaim the gospel should receive their livelihood from those who accept the gospel.

But I have never used any of these privileges, nor am I writing now to suggest that I should be given them. Indeed I would rather die than have anyone make this boast of mine an empty one!

The Treasurer of the Corinth Church to Paul

Dear Paul,

Our elders have accepted the condition contained in the Apostolic Decree that we should help to support the poor and needy in Jerusalem. That dreadful famine in Judaea makes us realize how fortunate we are here. And no doubt the great numbers of pilgrims who make their way to the Holy City must make great demands upon the hospitality of the Christians there. Some of our worldly-wise elders are wondering, however, whether the whole burden for this worthwhile cause will fall upon us, or whether other churches are also making their fair contributions? It is a reasonable question, for we cannot, alone, carry the whole cost. What, may we ask, is the present situation and how ought we to organize our appeal?

Sincerely,
David

P.S. Sorry we seem only to communicate with each other about money. But we can't do without it, even in the Church, can we?

Follow the Example of Macedonia

We must tell you about the grace that God has given to the Macedonian churches. Somehow, in most difficult circumstances, their joy and the fact of being down to their last penny themselves, produced a magnificent concern for other people. I can guarantee that they were willing to give to the limit of their means, yes, and beyond their means, without the slightest urging from me or anyone else. In fact they simply begged us to accept their gifts and so let them share the honor of supporting their brothers in Christ. Nor was their gift, as I must confess I had expected, a mere cash payment. Instead they made a complete dedication of themselves first to the Lord and then to us, as God's appointed ministers.

Now as far as the Fund for Christians in Need is concerned, I should like you to follow the same rule that I gave to the Galatian church.

On the first day of the week let everyone put so much by him, according to his financial ability, so that there will be no need for collections when I come. Then, on my arrival, I will send whomever you approve to take your gift, with my recommendation, to Jerusalem. If it seems right for me to go as well, we will make up a party together.

You were the first a year ago to think of helping, as well as to give, to carry through what you then intended to do. Finish it then, as well as you can, and show that you can complete what you set out to do with as much efficiency as you showed readiness to begin. After all, the important thing is to be willing to give so much as

*we can—that is what God accepts, and no one is asked
to give what he has not got.*

Paul was shrewd enough to recognize that money is a
means of communication. We say plenty both about ourselves and others by the causes to which we give our
money or from which we withhold it. Apart from the
alleviation of stark human need, Paul was hopeful that
the contributions made by Gentile churches to Jerusalem
would help to break down racial barriers and soften the
prejudice which some Jewish Christians felt against non-
Jews claiming to be part of the continuing church of
Israel.

Andrew Alias Plutus Alias Simeon to Paul

Reverend and Dear Sir,

You may remember I had cause to correspond with
you when I was Secretary of the Burglars' Guild concerning the question of the return of Our Lord and
the social implications of this belief in so far as and
for as much as my own profession is concerned. Whether
you did me the honor of replying to my letter I have no
way of knowing as I took a rather long holiday shortly
after I had written to you; well, to tell no lie and shame
the devil, I did a spell at sea, in the galleys. However,
I have now returned and have been most moved to hear
how the poor in Jerusalem have no food and you are
raising a fund to help them.

At a meeting of our guild on the 15th inst. this
matter was discussed in some detail and the following
resolution was passed *nem con.*—that 10 percent of our
net earnings before the shareout and after necessary
overheads have been paid should be handed over to
you for the benefit of all those poor people in Jerusalem
who must be so weak and hungry that they haven't the
strength to nick the purses of some of those big, fat

merchants of whom there is no shortage (so we are given to understand by our colleagues in that area).

I shall be most happy to meet you—preferably after dark in some suitable place—to hand over our first contribution. We ask nothing in return, except your prayers that nothing should prevent us from carrying on our profession, such as police, big dogs, or those newfangled locks the rich are importing from Rome.

> Yours most honestly,
> Andrew alias Plutus

How About Helping the Poor by the Wages of Honest Work?

If you used to be a thief you must not only give up stealing, but you must learn to make an honest living, so that you may be able to give to those in need.

Let there be no more foul language, but good words instead. Live your lives in love—the same sort of love which Christ gives us. But as for sexual immorality in all its forms and the itch to get your hands on what belongs to other people—don't even talk about such things. The keynote of your conversation should not be nastiness or silliness or flippancy, but a sense of all we owe to God. For of this much you can be quite certain: that neither the immoral nor the covetous man (which latter is, in effect, worshiping a false god) has any inheritance in the Kingdom of Christ and of God. Let your lives be living proofs of the things which please God. Steer clear of the activities of darkness, you know the sort of things I mean!

Barclaius, a Banker, to Paul

Dear Paul,

At the risk of being regarded as mean and unfeeling towards my fellow men, I write to protest against the raising of the Fund for Christians in Need. I most certainly have no objection to genuine charity, and indeed, without boasting, there are quite a number of families in this city who could testify to my generosity—but that is another matter. But do you not see that in handing out money to the so-called poor in Jerusalem we are, in my view, encouraging laziness and furthermore going against the ordinance of God who, in his infinite wisdom, has decreed that the rich and the poor are born as such and ought to remain in their respective states? I take equal objection to your constant harping on the fact that in Christ there is no male or female, bond or free, etc. Have you seriously thought through the consequences of such an irresponsible statement? God created Adam and Eve—that you cannot deny. If he had not intended that men and women should have different roles in life, then he would not have done it, would he? It is the same with this talk about there being no difference between slaves and freemen.

What are you—some Zealot revolutionary? Just as a donkey cannot become a horse or a black man change the color of his skin, so God, to whom be all praise, has created a world full of wonderful variety. No doubt there are compensations for being poor. Have you ever thought about that? No business worries. No sleepless nights, tossing in anguish about the possibility of wars, natural disasters, or even idiotic government policies wiping out the value of our currency. What do the poor know of such things? They just hold out their hands, and there are misguided people like yourself ready to fill their palms with money, money extracted from people like myself by what I do not hesitate to call moral blackmail.

In my view, the plight of the poor in Jerusalem is a matter for the imperial government—God knows they take enough from the taxpayer! Let them organize gangs to build roads or draft them into the army or something. There's nothing unchristian about that.

I cannot with a clear conscience contribute to this fund, and strongly object to the whole business. The sufficiency I possess I have earned. Let the lower orders do the same.

Indignantly,
Barclaius

The Gospel Is About Giving, Freely in Gratitude to God

All I will say is that poor sowing means a poor harvest, and a generous sowing means a generous harvest!

Let everyone give as his heart tells him, neither grudgingly nor under compulsion, for God loves the man whose heart is in his gift. After all, God can give you everything that you need, so that you may always have sufficient both for yourselves and for giving away to other people. As the Scripture says:

He hath scattered abroad, he hath given to the poor; his righteousness abides for ever.

He who gives the seed to the sower and turns that seed into bread to eat will give you the seed of generosity to sow and, for harvest, the satisfying bread of good deeds done. The more you are enriched by God the more scope will there be for generous giving, and your gifts, administered through us, will mean that many will thank God. For your giving does not end in meeting the wants of your fellow Christians. It also results in an overflowing tide of thanksgiving to God. Moreover, your very giving proves the reality of your faith, and that means that men thank God that you practice the gospel that you profess to believe in, as well as for the actual gifts you make to them.

Thank God, then, for his indescribable generosity to you!

For some reason or another, Paul has passed into Christian history and come down to us as a rather forbidding as well as a lonely figure. In fact, he seems to have had a genius both for making and keeping personal friends— just as he made enemies, unrelenting in their animosity towards him. In particular, he not only inspired younger men to heroic deeds for the gospel's sake, but has left no trace of jealousy at their success. He was sometimes let down by those he counted on for loyalty but in general he had the power to stiffen the backbone of the timid and imbue the fainthearted with some of his courage, so that they were proud to face hardship and opposition for his sake as well as the gospel's. He accepted at face value the reports of his emissaries and never hesitated to trust the most inexperienced colleague with an important assignment.

Take Titus. Paul sent him on difficult missions to Corinth and then left him behind in Crete to organize the church there. Titus, whom Paul called "my true son in the common faith," had a much more difficult task than that of Timothy, who had been entrusted with imposing some kind of order on the church at Ephesus. The Christian community in Crete was scattered to such a degree that it is stretching language to call the Cretan Christians a "church" at all. Equally, the opposition from Jews in Crete seems to have been particularly intense.

Titus to Paul

Reverend Sir,

How much longer must I stay in this God-forsaken spot? This place is a howling bedlam of argumentative, uncharitable ranters. I have known no place like it. When the so-called church gathers for worship, it is more like a marketplace with a multitude of self-styled teachers peddling their conflicting ideas, none of which seem to me to have much to do with the Christian faith. The Jews are the most vicious and divisive. They tell people that they ought not to listen to me because I have not been circumcised and so am an outsider— a semi-pagan who cannot be in the true tradition of Jesus, who was circumcised on the eighth day. They also spend hours reciting the genealogies of the Jewish faith, arguing about who begat who and in what order and claiming their own place in the true succession of the sons of Abraham. And their legends! Fanciful stories that have no spiritual value and recount the most weird and miraculous happenings which seem to me to have more in common with the mystery religions than with our common faith.

I am at my wits' end. I have tried to impose some order on our gatherings, but they shout me down and hurl abuse so vile that I truly believe that they are disciples of Satan rather than servants of Christ.

What am I to do? Please advise me.

Your son in Christ,
Titus

I Know Exactly What You Are Up Against

Mind you steer clear of stupid arguments, genealogies, controversies and quarrels over the law. They settle nothing and lead nowhere. There are many among the Jews who will not recognize authority, who talk nonsense and yet in so doing have managed to deceive men's minds. They must be silenced, for they have upset the faith of whole households, teaching what they have no business to teach for the sake of what they can get. One of them, yes, one of their prophets, has said: "Men of Crete are always liars, evil and beastly, lazy and greedy."

There is truth in this testimonial of theirs! Don't hesitate to reprimand them sharply, for you want them to be sound and healthy Christians, with a proper contempt for Jewish fairy tales and orders issued by men who have forsaken the path of truth.

Let your own life stand as a pattern of good living. In all your teaching show the strictest regard for truth and show you appreciate the seriousness of the matters you are dealing with. Your speech should be unaffected and logical, so that your opponent may feel ashamed at finding nothing in which to pick holes.

As soon as I send Artemas to you (or perhaps it will be Tychicus), do your best to come to me at Nicopolis, for I have made up my mind to spend the winter there.

Titus, Again to Paul

Father,

Artemas or Tychicus can't arrive quickly enough for me! I honestly feel I am wasting my time here. I have, since the first day you introduced me to Jesus, wished to be a missionary. But this is not missionary work; it is one long argument against men who are more cunning and fluent than I am. Nothing is sacred to these cynical debaters. Now they are questioning the Resurrection and claiming that the raising from the dead of Jesus by God is a past event and that the only way in which we shall also rise from the dead is by living on through our children and their children. Perhaps I lack the pastoral heart, but I long for nothing more than to move on, possibly to Dalmatia, where, God willing, people will be prepared to hear the good news and live as those who know and follow the Risen Lord.

I feel so defenseless.

A thoroughly demoralized
Titus

You Are Not Defenseless: These Are Your Weapons!

Put on God's complete armor so that you can success-fully resist all the devil's methods of attack. For, as I expect you have learned by now, our fight is not against any physical enemy: it is against organizations and powers that are spiritual. We are up against the unseen power that controls this dark world and spiritual agents from the very headquarters of evil. Therefore you must wear the whole armor of God that you may be able to resist evil in its day of power, and that even when you have fought to a standstill you may still stand your ground. Take your stand then with truth as your belt, righteousness your breastplate, the gospel of peace firmly on your feet, salvation as your helmet and in your hand the sword of the Spirit, the Word of God. Above all be sure you take faith as your shield, for it can quench every burning missile the enemy hurls at you. Pray at all times with every kind of spiritual prayer, keeping alert and persistent as you pray for all Christ's men and women. And pray for me, too, that I may be able to speak freely here, to make known the secret of the gospel for which I am, so to speak, an ambassador in chains.

Achim of Eliud to Paul

Dear Paul,

Titus has gone! Frankly, few of us here will be sorry. The pagans of Dalmatia are welcome to him. May we request that the next missionary you send us will have that authority which comes from a true blood line going back to Abraham, as I myself have. These things are so important. If we are truly the chosen people then we really must be sure of the ancestry of those who pre-sume to teach us. It takes only one half-breed (I'm thinking now of Timothy) to dilute our blood so that some day we shall no longer be able to keep ourselves separate and lose the covenant promise.

By the way, I note that you claim to be of the tribe of Benjamin. I have examined numerous scrolls which record the heredity of our people and there seems to be a gap in your genealogy around the time of Joram of Azariah. However, you can trust my discretion. Many of us have skeletons in our cupboards! Some of our forebears were a bit naughty at times. Let it be our little secret! Thank Jehovah you were circumcised! That puts the matter right.

Achim of Eliud

You Are Butchers Not Disciples

Let me repeat what I told the Christians at Philippi: Be on your guard against these curs, these wicked workmen, these would-be mutilators of your bodies! We are, remember, truly circumcised when we worship God by the Spirit, when we find our joy in Christ Jesus and put no confidence in what we are in the flesh.

I wish those who are so eager to cut your bodies would cut themselves off from you altogether!

So Titus left Crete and went northwards along the coast to Dalmatia, and from there he disappears into history. He was never so close to Paul as Timothy, but he was a genuine believer, a true missionary and did his best in an evil time to serve God. Legend has it that he returned to Crete and became bishop there; so at least Eusebius reports. There is no other corroboration of this fact. What is sure is that he did his duty as a faithful if undistinguished Christian—which makes him a fitting patron saint for most of us.

Then there was Demas.

Pilgrim's Regress

> *Demas and Luke are my fellow workers for God.*
> *Luke and Demas send you their best wishes.*
> *Demas has left me, having loved this present world.*
> *Only Luke is with me now.*

Demas to Paul

My dear Paul,

By the time you receive this letter I shall be with wife and family in Thessalonica. I'm afraid I can take no more. Unlike Luke and yourself, I am weary to the marrow of my bones with all the persecution and torment we have endured these past years. In spite of your handicap, you seem to be made of iron—prison, torture, hardship, constant harassment seem only to strengthen your resolve and make your faith burn all the brighter. I'm not made of any metal that is refined by fire; I warp and melt.

I wish with all my heart I could have stayed by your side, but you demanded too much of me, even though you were probably unaware of the fact. I am not the stuff of which missionary martyrs are made. Is that a terrible sin? Is it a crime to want a warm bed in which to sleep at night, regular meals, the love of a wife and family? Would Christ condemn me for that? Would Christ who had mercy on the penitent thief damn me for being unable to drink the cup that he drank?

Please pray for me. I am only capable of a little love, of a small sacrifice, of moderate hardship. Luke will care for you. In his gentle way he has your steadfastness. Pray for me because I am afraid of death and pain and loneliness. I ask your pardon and the forgiveness of

Christ. I am not worthy to be an apostle, but I shall continue to follow from a distance. But no more prison! No more controversy! No more endless journeys! I have come home, and here I want to stay.

Please don't think too badly of me. I have deserted you, but I hope I have not deserted Christ. It is just that my strength and endurance have deserted me. Possibly in time I shall regain them. Meanwhile, God grant you the companionship you deserve and which I was not able to give you.

Yours penitently,
Demas

Epaphras to Paul

My dear fellow prisoner,

Is it not ironic that you and I should find ourselves in jail for Christ's sake and yet have never met? It is even stranger that I came to Rome in order to consult you—and am the occupant of the next cell.

My concern is for a small group of Christians whom I have gathered together in Colossae—a town in the valley of Phrygia on the banks of the Lycus River. Colossae has been overshadowed in recent years by Hieropolis and Laodicea, but we were once an important center in Asia Minor.

I am neither an apostle nor a prophet as these terms are understood in Jerusalem, just an ordinary man who, having heard the good news, was filled with the Spirit and took it back to Colossae. Now we are a thriving fellowship. But I have a problem which is beyond my spiritual and intellectual powers to cope with—angels! Yes, angels. I had preached to the best of my ability the Cross of Jesus and its effect upon our daily lives. I'm afraid that it was only half a gospel I gave them.

Most of those who heard me accepted what I said, but they (as I now see) merely added Jesus to the angelic beings whom they had believed in before they heard of him.

I need not spell out to someone of your knowledge and experience what a dangerous situation has been created by the belief of the people in a strange mixture of the old fantasies and the new gospel.

I'm sure your authority and expository skill are needed to halt the spawning of a sub-Christian community with all its attendant vices. At all costs, the lordship of Christ must be proclaimed in its fullness to subdue these elemental powers which have such a grip on the lives of the peoples of Asia Minor. What I am pleading for is a letter from you, taken by either Tychicus or Onesimus—who is greatly loved in Colossae —to set matters right.

I know my appeal will not fall on deaf ears. I look forward to meeting you. The chances seem good, since you are almost within reach of my outstretched arm!

> Yours respectfully,
> Epaphras

Encouragement and Affirmation

I want you to know by this letter that we here are constantly praying for you, and whenever we do we thank God the Father because you believe in Christ and because you are showing Christian love towards other Christians. Wherever that gospel goes, it produces Christian character, and develops it, as it has done in your own case from the time you first heard and realized the amazing fact of God's grace.

You learned these things, we understand, from Epaphras, who is of the same service as we are. He is a most well-loved minister of Christ, and has your well-being very much at heart.

Now Christ is the visible expression of the invisible God. He existed before creation began, for it was through him that everything was made. He is, therefore, justly called the Lord of all. It was in him that the full nature of God chose to live, and through him God planned to reconcile in his own person, as it were, everything on earth and everything in heaven by virtue of the sacrifice of the Cross. Yet is in him that God gives a full and complete expression of himself (within the limits that he set himself in Christ). Moreover, your own completeness is only realized in him, who is the authority over all authorities, and the supreme power over all powers.

If anything demonstrates Paul's exquisite tact, this letter does. He does not begin by thundering denunciation upon the heads of these Colossian Christians for their mistaken and semipagan notions. He wins their sympathetic attention by congratulating them for the degree of Christian faith they have achieved and assures them of his prayerful understanding. Nor does he dismiss with contempt the philosophy of life the gospel is replacing. Instead, he incorporates the belief of the ancient world in cosmic powers into a theology of history which is centered in the Cross but has both its origin and goal in a Christ whose redemptive work embraces both earth and heaven. He makes it impossible for them to relegate Christ to the role of one angelic being among many, by elevating him to the unique position of universal Creator and Judge.

Thank God for a Good Leader!

Epaphras, one of you, and a real servant of Christ, sends his greeting. He works hard for you even here,

for he prays constantly and earnestly for you, that you
may become mature Christians, and may fulfill God's
plans for you. From my own observation, I can tell you
that he has a real passion for your welfare, and for that
of the churches at Laodicea and Hieropolis.

A Laodicean to Paul

Dear Paul,

Your letter to the Colossian Christians was passed
on to us here since Epaphras also keeps a fatherly eye
on us. I feel I ought, in Christian love, to tell you what
he himself would not out of loyalty to a fellow elder
reveal. One Archippus was ordained to be our local
minister and is proving to be a problem. To put it
bluntly, he is lazy and self-indulgent. His sermons are
badly and hastily prepared, and he visits only the more
influential and wealthy members of our congregation,
and even then to enjoy their lavish hospitality rather
than to speak to them of spiritual things. He gives the
deacons so little supervision that they too are beginning
to follow his example, with the result that the poor and
sick are not properly cared for. His hobby is fishing in
the Lycus, and he seems to rejoice more in a catch
which has fins and scales than in his first duty—to be,
as our Lord taught, a fisher of men.

I take no pleasure in reporting this matter to you.
But I am afraid that the state of the whole church has
become lukewarm and lacking in zeal, and that the
fire of the Spirit has almost gone out. We make no converts and those we have we are losing for lack of teaching and discipline.

I write because I am jealous of the good name of
Laodicea and would not wish it to become notorious in
the Christian world for its lack of devotion to Christ.

Nymphas, an Elder

Straight from the Shoulder

A brief message to Archippus: God ordained you to your work—see that you don't fail him!

Nymphas' fears were well-founded, for the next time we read of the church at Laodicea in the Bible it is in the Revelation of John, and it has become immortalized as being neither hot nor cold, and therefore spewed out of God's mouth—a damning indictment, if ever there was one. What degree of blame falls to Archippus it is impossible at this distance in time to judge. But the warning is there—the seeds of indolence and spiritual languor already sown in the lifetime of the apostle were to produce a dreadful harvest, decades later.

An Elder of the Roman Church to Paul

My dear Paul,

I left you after my visit to you in jail with a profound sense of unease. We in Rome had thought our reception of you was cordial and respectful. But it seems that there are those among us who, for reasons I prefer not to probe, resent your presence here—even though you are denied your freedom. In public, all Christians, except for a handful of Judaizers, speak well of you, but it is obvious that there is an underground movement against you. In my eyes, you are the greatest of all the apostles because you had the hardest task—to preach the gospel of a Jew, executed by Gentiles, to the pagan world.

It is not from anything you actually said that I got the impression that you are being scorned and derided. You just seemed depressed not about your captivity (you triumph gloriously over that!) but about the gossip and rumor which finds its way somehow through the prison walls and adds to your torment. Am I right, or just imagining things? I must know, because if so, our church is diseased, and the canker must be cut out before it infects us all and destroys our fellowship.

Mandus Tactus

I Have Learned to Live with Disloyalty

I know that some are preaching Christ out of jealousy, in order to annoy me, but some are preaching him in good faith. The motive of the former is questionable— they preach in a partisan spirit, hoping to make my chains even more galling than they would otherwise be. But what does it matter? However they look at it, the fact remains that Christ is being preached, whether sincerely or not, and that fact makes me very happy. The first time I had to defend myself no one was on my side—they all deserted me, God forgive them! Yet the Lord himself stood by me and gave me the strength to proclaim the message clearly and fully, so that the Gentiles could hear it, and I was rescued "from the lion's mouth." I am sure the Lord will rescue me from every evil plot, and will keep me safely until I reach his heavenly Kingdom. Glory be to him for ever and ever!

Mandus Tactus Again, to Paul

Dear Paul,

It is just as I suspected! Well, I promise you that I and the Elders who hold you in such veneration will root out traitors and fair-weather Christians without mercy! You have suffered enough. The tragedy is that there is no shortage of "little" men, puffed up with a sense of their own importance, who cannot bear to hear you, your exploits and teaching spoken of with such great respect. I have confided in some of my brethren and they are as angry as I am. We shall purge our church of such unchristian deeds and sentiments even though we lose half our number. Do not fear. We shall vindicate you!

Mandus Tactus

No! Christian Love Must Bind Together Not Divide

What we need is a genuine break with evil and a real devotion to good. Let us have real warm affection for one another as between brothers, and a willingness to let the other man have the credit. Let us not allow slackness to spoil our work and let us keep the fires of the spirit burning, as we do our work for God. As for those who try to make your lives a misery, bless them. Don't curse, bless. Share the happiness of those who are happy, and the sorrow of those who are sad. Live in harmony with each other. Don't become set in your own opinions. Don't pay back a bad turn by a bad turn, to anyone. As far as your responsibility goes, live in peace with everyone. Never take vengeance into your own hands.

Christ is our living peace. He has made a unity of the conflicting elements of Jew and Gentile by breaking down the barrier which lay between us. By his sacrifice he removed the hostility of the law, with all its commandments and rules, and made in himself out of the two, Jew and Gentile, one new man, thus producing peace. So you are no longer outsiders or aliens, but fellow citizens with every other Christian—we belong now to the household of God. You are all part of this building in which God himself lives by his Spirit.

It is doubtful whether Paul really believed that his spell in prison, which ended with his death by decapitation around A.D. 65, was the terminus of his earthly road. He had many narrow escapes from death and possibly hoped that he would regain his freedom to preach the gospel in regions hitherto beyond his reach. As he told the Philippians:

I Doubt I Have Reached the End of the Road Yet

The work I have started may make it necessary for me to go on living in this world. I should find it very hard to make a choice. I am torn in two directions— on the one hand I long to leave this world and live with Christ, and that is obviously the best thing for me. Yet, on the other hand, it is probably more necessary for you that I should stay here on earth but shall be able to stand by you, to help you forward in Christian living and to find increasing joy in your faith. So you can look forward to making much of me as your minister in Christ when I come to see you again!

As time wore on, Paul, probably sensing his imminent death, turned in his desolation to his young convert, Timothy, and in what may be a final declaration, ends with a very human request:

Paul to Timothy

I feel that the last drops of my life are being poured out for God. The glorious fight God gave me I have fought, the course that I was set I have finished, and I have kept the faith. The future for me holds the crown of righteousness which God, the true judge, will give

to me in that day—and not, of course, only to me but
to all those who have loved what they have seen of him.
Do your best to come to me as soon as you can.
Do your best to get here before the winter.

His end seems full of pathos. He has only three close
friends, his unseen Master, Luke, his physician, and the
young half-caste, Timothy. The first two were with him
constantly; Timothy he urges to come "before winter"
because the gale-swept Mediterranean became unnavigable
once the summer ended. And Paul asks only that Timothy
should bring with him his travel-stained robe and his
books. Whether Timothy reached him we shall never know.
Paul's end is obscured by legend. Even the date of his
death is uncertain. All we know is that he was executed by
decapitation on the orders of the Emperor Nero. And it is
said that he died at Aqua Salviae on the road to Ostia.

The old warhorse, who on first acquaintance seems
somewhat austere and forbidding, was to become, after
Jesus, the greatest figure in the history of the Christian
Church; its greatest missionary; its supreme strategist; and
the one who transformed what might have turned in-
wards upon itself, as a Jewish cult, into a world religion.
Not a bad record for a Jewish tentmaker!